Cadbury's
THE TASTE
of
CHOCOLATE

PATRICIA DUNBAR

MARTIN BOOKS

Published by Martin Books
Simon & Schuster International Group
Fitzwilliam House
32 Trumpington Street
Cambridge CB2 1QY

in association with
Cadbury Ltd
PO Box 12
Bournville
Birmingham B30 2LU

First published 1990
© Cadbury Ltd, 1990
All rights reserved

ISBN 0 85941 660 7

Design: Patrick McLeavey & Partners
Food preparation for photography: Julia Wicks, Michele Crisp
    and Frances Vines
Illustration: John Hutchinson
Typesetting: Goodfellow & Egan Ltd, Cambridge
Printed and bound in Spain by Cayfosa, Barcelona

Photographs
Cadbury Ltd photographic studio (**Richard London** and
Manvir Rai), all photographs except pages 17, 25, 37, 41, 43, 63,
77, 79, 81, 85, 111 and 119 by **Gina Harris** and pages 31, 46, 55,
59, 89, 102, 103, 105 and 107 by
David Miles.

ACKNOWLEDGEMENTS
This book would not have been possible without all the hard work
and long hours put into developing and testing the recipes by the
team of Cadbury home economists, past and present; in particular
Julia Wicks, Sheelin Davies and Michele Crisp, ably assisted by
Wendy Nicholls, with Sheila Sayers helping in the department.
I should also like to thank Jan Jones who cheerfully typed most of
the manuscript – thank you all.
    I owe an enormous debt of gratitude to Helen Botfield who
wrote the introduction on the history of chocolate, has worked
with us for over ten years and has been a constant source of
inspiration and support.

CADBURY TRADE MARKS
References in this book to Cadbury trade marks denote the use of
the following products in the recipes:
CADBURY'S FLAKE – Chocolate bar
DAIRY MILK – Milk chocolate
BOURNVITA – Malted chocolate drink granules
BOURNVILLE – Cocoa or plain chocolate as indicated
CADBURY'S BUTTONS – Chocolate drops

NOTES ON RECIPES
Use *either* metric *or* imperial measurements. Never mix the two as
they are not interchangeable.

Exact metric/imperial equivalents are given for cans and dairy
products where these are given on the packaging. In other
instances, handy conversions are used.

All spoon measures are level unless otherwise stated.

Baking tins Although it is preferable to use the size stated, the
exact-sized tin may sometimes not be available. The capacity of a
round cake tin equals that of a square one which is 2.5 cm (1 inch)
smaller. Cake tins can be adjusted by 1.5 cm (½ inch) without any
adverse effects, but keep an eye on cooking times.

All the recipes have been well tested in the Cadbury home
economics department.

Contents

The Story of Cadbury's Chocolate

The origins of chocolate can be traced back to the Aztec and Mayan civilisations in Central America. Reputedly, Christopher Columbus introduced the cocoa bean to Europe, but in fact it was his fellow explorer, the Spanish Conquistador Don Cortez, who first realised its commercial value.

When Don Cortez discovered Mexico City, capital of the Aztecs, in 1519, he is said to have been introduced to the spicy drink known as *chocolatl* by Emperor Montezuma himself. This thick, rich drink, made from ground cocoa beans, mixed with maize meal and flavoured with vanilla and chilli, had been consumed in the area for hundreds of years.

When Cortez brought the cocoa beans back to Spain, the flavour of the drink was improved by heating it and adding sugar. The way in which it was prepared was kept a closely guarded secret for almost a century.

The custom of drinking chocolate eventually spread to England in the mid seventeenth century, but it was a very expensive luxury. When the first 'Chocolate Houses' opened in London in 1657, chocolate cost the equivalent of 50–75 pence a pound, when the pound sterling was worth considerably more than it is today.

The Chocolate Houses sold chocolate as a drink and also a pressed cake from which the drink could be made in the home. Chocolate remained a luxury until 1853, when Gladstone's government reduced the very heavy import duty.

THE ONE-MAN BUSINESS

93 Bull Street, a one-man grocery business opened in 1824 in a fashionable shopping area of Birmingham, was the foundation of Cadbury Ltd; today Cadbury are one of the world's largest producers of chocolate. The young Quaker, John Cadbury, was twenty-two years old when he opened his shop to sell not only tea but coffee, hops, mustard and two new side-lines – cocoa and drinking chocolate – which he prepared himself using a mortar and pestle.

By 1831 he had become a manufacturer of cocoa and drinking chocolate, with a warehouse in Crooked Lane, Birmingham. The earliest cocoas were 'balanced' with potato starch and sago flour to 'absorb' the excess cocoa butter, plus other ingredients designed to give healthy properties to the drinks. The earliest preserved price list of 1842 shows that John Cadbury sold sixteen lines of drinking chocolate in cake and powder with names such as Churchman's Chocolate and Fine Brown Chocolate, plus eleven lines of cocoa including Granulated Cocoa and Homeopathic Cocoa, in addition to French eating chocolate.

1853 saw the first Royal Warrant being awarded as manufacturers of cocoa and chocolate to Queen Victoria, and the company has held Royal Warrants of Appointment ever since. In 1861, John Cadbury retired, handing over the business to his sons, Richard and George. These two Cadbury brothers, particularly George, were the cornerstones of this family business which was to grow into an internationally renowned company. In addition to a large number of manufacturing developments, the brothers introduced industrial and social reforms, setting a pattern to be followed by many other large companies.

COCOA ESSENCE — 'ABSOLUTELY PURE'

A major technical advance that changed the face of chocolate and cocoa production was brought to England in 1866 by the Cadbury brothers. A process first developed in Holland for pressing cocoa butter from cocoa beans was introduced and cocoa essence, forerunner of today's cocoa, was produced. The resulting drink was less rich and much more palatable, so there was no need to add the various types of flour and starch. Cadbury's new cocoa essence was advertised as 'Absolutely Pure — Therefore Best.'

The plentiful supply of cocoa butter that remained after the cocoa was pressed enabled chocolate-making as we know it today to be developed. Eating chocolate first appeared on the Cadbury listings in the 1840s but this was very different to the chocolate we now enjoy. When the extra cocoa butter was added to the basic ingredients, cocoa nib and sugar, the chocolate became easier to mould into bars with a good appearance and

Opposite and above: a selection of very attractive Cadbury packaging from various eras.

texture, or to use for covering other confections.

From the mid 1860s onwards, Cadbury introduced many new kinds of eating chocolate: refined forms of plain chocolate, plus fruit-flavoured centres covered with chocolate and sold in delightfully decorated boxes. Many early boxes were designed by Richard Cadbury himself, sometimes using his children as models and sometimes depicting flowers or scenes from holiday journeys. The increasingly elaborate chocolate boxes, whose designs ranged from superb velvet-covered caskets with bevelled mirrors and silk linings to pretty boxes with delightful pictures of kittens, flowers, landscapes and attractive girls, were very popular with the Victorians.

The first chocolate Easter Eggs made by Cadbury were produced in 1875. These early eggs were made of 'dark' chocolate with a plain, smooth surface and were filled with dragées. The earliest 'decorated eggs' had plain shells with chocolate piping and marzipan flowers.

1879: THE MOVE TO BOURNVILLE

Increasing success meant that factory space in central Birmingham was outgrown. A 14½-acre 'greenfield site' with a trout stream running through and a solitary building – Bournbrook Cottage – was chosen. At this time the French led the confectionery business, so a French-sounding name was deemed appropriate. 'Bourn', taken from Bournbrook, was added to the word *ville* (French for town) and 'Bournville' was born.

The development of the Bournville 'factory in a garden', the village of Bournville with its educational, social and sports amenities, together with the then revolutionary conditions for employees have gone down in social history as models for future generations.

Among the many innovations in the new factory was the appointment in 1880 of M. Frederic Kinchelman, a master-confectioner from the Continent, who brought the secrets of the French confectioners to Bournville. Delicacies such as nougats, *pistache*, *pâte d'abricot*, and avelines were soon produced.

CADBURY'S DAIRY MILK

Before 1900, a very coarse and dry milk chocolate was made by adding milk powder paste to the basic chocolate recipe. Swiss chocolate, superior in taste and texture, dominated the market.

George Cadbury Junior set out to challenge this

Beautiful boxes have always been a feature of Cadbury's range.

domination. By 1905 a new milk chocolate made with fresh milk was ready, and it was not merely 'as good as' but better than the imported chocolate. Three names were considered – 'Jersey', 'Highland Milk' and 'Dairy Maid', which became 'Dairy Milk' – and a new star chocolate brand was launched. Cadbury's Dairy Milk was a success story that has continued to this day.

Bournville plain chocolate, a semi-sweet smooth dark chocolate, was introduced in 1908 as the perfect partner for Cadbury's Dairy Milk. Bournville is not only delicious to eat, it is also the best chocolate to use for that wonderful chocolate taste in cakes and desserts.

Recipes for Cadbury's Dairy Milk, Bournville chocolate and many other famous Cadbury brands have remained largely the same since they were first introduced. Refinements have taken place, many new products have been introduced and there have been tremendous technological advances in production.

Cadbury is a pre-eminent name in confectionery world-wide. Many brand names are the same throughout the world, but recipes may vary according to local tastes, eating habits, climate conditions and ingredients available. But wherever you buy your bar of chocolate you can be sure that it will be of the same high quality that has been demanded since the very early days of Cadbury chocolate production.

How Chocolate is Made

Cocoa beans from the tree *Theobroma cacao* (illustrated right) are the basis of chocolate and cocoa. Although a native of the Amazon basin and other tropical areas of South and Central America, where wild varieties are still found in the forests, the cocoa tree is now grown in a number of countries which have humid tropical climates with regular rains and a short dry season.

West Africa is the major producer, with Ghana growing the best-quality cocoa in the world, for which a premium is paid. Other cocoa-growing areas are Central and South America and the Far East. Cadbury purchase their cocoa beans almost exclusively from Ghana, buying the world's best quality raw material to guarantee the Cadbury taste and quality.

Cocoa farming is a small, unsophisticated, family business in Ghana, and the planting patterns of the cocoa fields make mechanisation impractical. In Ghana, cocoa trees are best grown shaded from direct sun and wind, particularly in the early stages of growth. There are two general methods for establishing cocoa: sometimes young trees are interspersed with new permanent and temporary shade trees, such as coconut, plantains and bananas, following clear-

felling; alternatively, existing forest is thinned before cocoa trees are planted between the established trees.

Cocoa trees resemble English apple trees, seldom reaching more than 7.5 metres (25 feet) high. The flowers and pods grow directly out from the trunk and branches. Flowers can be present throughout the year but appear in abundance just after the onset of the rain. October to December is the main harvesting period in West Africa.

Fermentation is essential to remove the pulp and astringency of the bean and to develop the true chocolate flavour. In Ghana, cocoa beans are piled up on a layer of large banana leaves with more banana leaves and stems on top and they are left for 5–6 days, being turned once to ensure even fermentation. During fermentation, the sugar in the pulp turns to alcohol and vinegar-like liquids, which drain away, and the temperature rises to 50°C. The beans are then slowly dried, spread out on mats raised off the ground, which gives superior flavour.

Dry, fermented beans are packed into sacks and stored in dockside warehouses ready to ship. All beans used by Cadbury in the United Kingdom go to a modern processing plant at Chirk in North Wales.

THE COCOA FACTORY

Sorting and cleaning are the first steps in processing the cocoa beans at the factory. Beans are cracked and broken and the shells are removed in the 'winnowing' process; the shell is blown away by air currents, leaving broken pieces of cocoa bean known as 'nibs'.

Roasting of the nibs takes place in revolving drums heated to a temperature of 135°C. This completes the development of the chocolate flavour, a process which started on the plantation when the beans were fermented. The roasting-time depends on whether the end use is for cocoa powder or for chocolate.

Nibs are ground in steel pin mills until the friction and heat of milling reduces them to a thick chocolate-coloured liquid called 'mass' or 'liquor', which contains 55–58% cocoa butter and solidifies on cooling. Cocoa powder and chocolate production now diverge.

Cocoa powder is made by extracting under pressure about half the cocoa butter, which is later used in chocolate-making. The amount of cocoa butter removed is specified in United Kingdom food laws.

The resulting solid block of cocoa, known as 'press', is ground and reground into a fine, high-grade cocoa powder. Drinking chocolate has sugar added to the cocoa; malted drinks include malt extract.

CHOCOLATE PRODUCTION

Cadbury make a variety of chocolates for different purposes, but the two main types are Cadbury's 'Bournville' plain chocolate and Cadbury's 'Dairy Milk' milk chocolate.

When plain chocolate is made, the 'mass' goes straight to the Bournville factory in Birmingham. 'Mass' for milk chocolate is first taken to the Cadbury milk factory at Marlbrook, where it is mixed with fresh, full-cream milk and high-grade sugar, condensed into a rich, creamy liquid and then dried to give milk chocolate 'crumb'. This is taken to Cadbury factories at Bournville, Birmingham and Somerdale, Bristol to continue the process. The addition of fresh milk is a traditional Cadbury technique; most other milk chocolate is made with dried milk powder.

At the chocolate factory, 'crumb' is pulverised and ground, and cocoa butter (extracted when making cocoa powder) is added. The amount of fat (cocoa butter) added depends on the consistency of the chocolate required; thick chocolate is needed for moulded bars; a thinner consistency is needed for chocolate used for assortments and covered bars. In the United Kingdom, up to 5% vegetable fat is added to compensate for variations in cocoa butter, so that the melting properties of the chocolate are controlled to a precise standard. The vegetable fats used by Cadbury are carefully selected to be similar in nature to cocoa butter.

Both milk chocolate and plain chocolate, which has had sugar and cocoa butter added to the mass before grinding, undergo the same final special production stages.

The most important component of chocolate, as far as texture is concerned, is the fat; the special processes of 'conching' and 'tempering' are controlled to produce chocolate with the fat in a specific physical structure.

'Conching' involves mixing the semi-liquid mixture, developing the flavour, removing unwanted volatile flavours and reducing the viscosity of the chocolate.

'Tempering' is the final, crucial stage, which in simple terms involves mixing and cooling the liquid chocolate under carefully controlled conditions to ensure that the chocolate has the right texture. Without tempering, the chocolate would be very soft and it would not have the lovely gloss and snap that is characteristic of chocolate.

THE END PRODUCT

To make bars of solid chocolate, known as moulded products, tempered liquid chocolate is poured into bar-shaped moulds, shaken and cooled before continuing to high-speed wrapping plants.

In 'countline products' like Crunchie or Double Decker, the chocolate covers the centre filling. Chocolate assortments may be made by the 'shelling' process, used for creams and novelties, where liquid chocolate is deposited in a mould to form a shell into which the centre is put, followed by the 'back'. More solid centres such as caramel, coconut and fudge are covered by the 'enrobing' method, where the centres pass on a continuous belt beneath a curtain of liquid chocolate. Easter Eggs are also made by the 'shell' process, with just the initial chocolate shell being used, except for Cadbury's Creme Eggs, which have the special 'yolk and white' filling. Special processes have been developed for products like Wispa, and for Spira with its unique twisted shape.

NEW TECHNOLOGY

Cadbury's chocolate production is a highly sophisticated, computer-controlled process, with much of the new specialist machinery being produced to Cadbury's own design and specification. The new Creme Egg plant at Bournville produces 66,000 Creme Eggs per hour, and has an overall capacity of 370 million eggs per year. 70,000 Wispa bars are produced every hour and 1.3 million Cadbury's Milk Chocolate Buttons are made per hour on a new plant. Each week the Bournville site alone produces 1,200 tonnes of chocolate — 1.6 million bars of various kinds plus 50 million Hazelnut Whirls and other individual chocolates.

Cadbury branded products used in this book.

CADBURY WORLD

Such is the fascination with the magical story of chocolate and the growth of Cadbury that a new visitor's centre has been opened on the Bournville factory site in Birmingham. 'Cadbury World' is the true Chocolate Experience. Visitors can immerse themselves in every aspect of the story, from the Aztecs in sixteenth-century Central America, to tasting the early chocolate drinks, through the Chocolate Houses of Georgian England, followed by the growth of Cadbury from the pioneering days of George and Richard Cadbury right up to modern, high-technology production and marketing techniques.

A demonstration production line shows the special Cadbury World chocolate assortment completing the journey from cocoa bean to chocolate, with a chance to sample the product along the way! Cadbury World caters for parties and family groups alike, as there is a wealth of interest for everyone.

Chocolate in Cooking

Not only is chocolate a favourite confectionery product, it is also undoubtedly one of the most popular flavours in cooking. Ask anyone which dessert or cake they would choose as a celebration, and nine times out of ten it would be a chocolate speciality!

Successful chocolate recipes depend on a good-quality chocolate; the discerning cook will always use a dessert chocolate such as Cadbury's Bournville although it may be slightly more difficult to handle.

Cadbury's Bournville, which is semi-sweet dessert plain chocolate, is ideal for all aspects of cookery as it gives a rich chocolate flavour. Some recipes are made with Cadbury's Dairy Milk milk chocolate and they will be a little sweeter and lighter in colour. When it comes to melting and re-setting the chocolate as a cake icing, however, plain chocolate is the one to choose.

United Kingdom food laws are quite specific about what can and cannot be called 'chocolate', but the term is quite often inaccurately used by consumers. Chocolate is any product obtained from cocoa nib, cocoa mass, cocoa, fat-reduced cocoa or any combination of two or more of these, with or without extracted cocoa butter and sucrose. Plain chocolate must not contain less than 30% total dry cocoa solids, of which 12% must be non-fat cocoa solids and not less than 18% cocoa butter. Milk chocolate contains a minimum of 14% milk solids (20% in Cadbury's milk chocolate), and less cocoa solids.

Chocolate is a recipe product and within the broad legal framework its composition varies by brand, for example the cocoa solids which give the chocolate its rich flavour differ according to the special brand taste. Continental chocolate has higher levels of cocoa solids and therefore tends to have a much stronger flavour.

The range of products popularly known as 'cooking chocolates' are in fact chocolate substitutes, which should be called 'chocolate-flavoured' cake coverings. These products contain cocoa solids but not cocoa butter. Instead they are made from other fats which do not need to be tempered, making them easier to melt. In flavour and texture terms, there is no comparison. A compound chocolate *couverture* is used in catering, but needs tempering before use so is unsuitable for home use.

Cocoa is an economical way of achieving a good chocolate flavour in everyday recipes and is used in mixtures which are thoroughly cooked, such as cakes, biscuits, puddings and sauces. When recipes have a high proportion of starch ingredients, cocoa is usually sieved with the dry ingredients. In other recipes, the cocoa is cooked by mixing the cocoa powder to a thick paste with boiling water. Drinking chocolate may be used to produce a milder, sweeter flavour, but allowance must be made within the recipe for the extra sugar included as part of drinking chocolate.

Cadbury's Flake, renowned as the perfect partner

for ice cream, is an invaluable milk chocolate cooking ingredient. Delicious as a decoration, Cadbury's Flake used in pieces in the recipe itself adds a lovely crunch to the cake or dessert. Cadbury's milk chocolate Buttons and the new creamy-white Buttons are wonderful for decoration, particularly children's novelty cakes and other goodies. Gently rubbing the Buttons between the thumb and forefinger gives you that lovely glossy surface.

HANDLING PLAIN CHOCOLATE

Careful handling when *melting chocolate* will prevent problems. Some people find it difficult to melt dessert chocolates of any kind and even write to say that the recipe must have been changed, which is certainly not the case with Cadbury chocolate. There are really two things of importance when melting chocolate: do not overheat, and do not be in a hurry.

Plain chocolate is generally easier to use in cookery than milk chocolate, which has a higher fat content and tends to burn more easily. Break the chocolate into a bowl or on to a plate and place it over a pan of hot, not boiling, water so that it is not touching the water and there is no chance of steam escaping and touching the chocolate. Take the pan off the heat and leave the chocolate for 10 minutes or so for a 200 g bar of Cadbury's Bournville chocolate. The 50 g bar will take slightly less time.

Leave the chocolate alone, do not attempt to stir it until it is quite soft. It will retain its shape though, and the centre of each block stays quite hard until the last minute. When soft all the way through, stir the chocolate and use as required, avoiding working it more than absolutely necessary. Once melted, use immediately; standing the bowl in a warm place is usually enough to keep the chocolate soft, though.

Another way to melt chocolate is in a microwave

Cadbury products are marvellous for decorations.

cooker but again care must be taken not to burn it. Break up the chocolate into a pint-size bowl then microwave on DEFROST for 3 or 4 minutes, depending on the thickness of the bar used. The lumps of chocolate will still appear to be whole but will be soft right through when it is ready. Leave them to continue melting, stirring only occasionally to produce the smooth glossy liquid chocolate. Do not be tempted to re-heat as the chocolate is likely to crystallise and burn.

Cream should be melted with the chocolate, while butter should be added to the chocolate immediately on melting. Added ingredients with a high water or liquid content should be avoided unless they are heated with the chocolate right from the beginning.

When the melted chocolate has been used to cover a gâteau or for decorations, the chocolate should be left to set in a cool dry place, not the refrigerator.

What went wrong?

Difficulties can occur because the carefully controlled tempering of the original manufacture can be destroyed if chocolate is melted for culinary use at home without due care. None of these problems should occur if the melting tips are carefully followed.

Scorching or burning is caused by excessive heat, resulting in a burnt taste and damage to the components of the chocolate, so that the texture becomes gritty.

Thickening of liquid chocolate to a solid mass may be due to: uneven heating or over-heating; the subsequent addition of other ingredients with high water contents that upset the balance; spillage of water from the saucepan. This is, regrettably, irreversible.

'Bloom' when melted chocolate sets is caused by: destroying the temper; the effects of moisture from steam when chocolate is melted over a pan of water; cooling rapidly in a 'damp' place such as the refrigerator; over heating; or the addition of fats which do not mix with cocoa butter. Although unsightly, the whitish spots and mottled appearance which develop with 'bloom' are *not* signs of chocolate 'going off', and the chocolate is quite edible because flavour is not affected, although the appearance is spoilt. A short-term remedy is to brush with milk just before serving.

Fig. 1

Fig. 2

Finishing Touches

Chocolate decorations on a cake, dessert or gâteau are the final touches which make a recipe look really special. Those attractive chocolate curls, leaves, shapes of all descriptions, squares or triangles which look so professional are in fact quite simple to make using Cadbury's Bournville chocolate. Once made, they can be stored in an airtight container for a limited period.

Chocolate curls are very easy and the best effect is obtained by scraping a swivel vegetable peeler along the flat side of a large bar of Cadbury's Bournville chocolate, shaving it off in curls as large or as fat as you need (see the photograph on page 11). The chocolate should be at room temperature. Alternatively, grate the chocolate coarsely.

Chocolate leaves are extremely decorative and useful to have on hand. Choose unblemished rose or bay leaves and then wipe clean and dry thoroughly. Melt some Bournville chocolate; when absolutely smooth, coat the underneath (veined) side of each leaf, either by carefully dragging it through the chocolate or by brushing it evenly. Leave to set. Later, gently *peel the leaf away* from the chocolate, *not* the other way round (Fig. 2). Store in a cool place ready to use.

Chocolate squares are made by spreading melted chocolate into a rectangle on a laminated plastic or marble board and allowing it to set. Mark even-sized squares using a ruler, then cut with a sharp knife. Squares can be cut diagonally for triangles. (See the photograph on page 13.)

For other decorations which need to be piped, use a small greaseproof paper piping bag, made to double thickness (page 15), then if the chocolate hardens in the bag it can be softened again in the microwave (providing a metal pipe is not included!) or a warm place. Cutting the tip off the bag is often all that is needed, as icing pipes tend to clog up with chocolate rather quickly.

Chocolate shapes are effective and not difficult to make. Trace outlines of your chosen shapes on to plain paper, and then lay a sheet of waxed or baking paper on top. Pipe over each shape with melted chocolate, filling in the centres. When completely set, pull off the paper carefully. (See the photograph opposite.)

Cadbury's Flake, milk chocolate Buttons and creamy-white Buttons are effective decorations. Crushed Cadbury's Flake makes an easy coating for the side of a cake and all sorts of interesting designs can be made on the top using a template of an animal, tree or name surrounded by crushed Flake. Both Cadbury's Flake and Buttons are invaluable for novelty cakes. In the following pages you will find lots of ideas to make your chocolate dishes look really superb.

Melted chocolate has a wide variety of decorative uses.

AMERICAN AND AUSTRALIAN CONVERSION CHART

	BRITISH	AMERICAN	AUSTRALIAN
Teaspoons and tablespoons	1 teaspoon (5 ml)	1 teaspoon (5 ml)	1 teaspoon (5 ml)
	*1 tablespoon	1 rounded tablespoon	1 scant tablespoon
	2 tablespoons	2 tablespoons	1½ tablespoons
	3 tablespoons	3 tablespoons	2½ tablespoons
	4 tablespoons	4 tablespoons	3½ tablespoons
	5 tablespoons	5 tablespoons	4½ tablespoons
†*Cup measures – liquid*	4 tablespoons	¼ cup	¼ cup
	125 ml (4 fl oz)	½ cup	½ cup
	250 ml (8 fl oz)	1 cup	1 cup
	450 ml (¾ pint)	2 cups	2 cups
	568 ml (1 pint)	2½ cups	2½ cups

All spoon measures are level unless otherwise stated.

*British standard tablespoons = 17.5 ml; American standard tablespoon = 14.2 ml; Australian standard tablespoon = 20 ml.
†American measuring cup = 250 ml (8 fl oz); Australian measuring cup = 250 ml (8 fl oz). (Note: British pint = 20 fl oz; American pint = 16 fl oz; Australian pint = 20 fl oz)

Back to Basics

Cookery is not an exact science and it is therefore important to use the senses: a recipe that *looks* appealing somehow always *tastes* better too. We have used some food colourings in our recipes, but these can generally be omitted if wished, except when, for example, a 'blue sea' is called for on a novelty cake.

The *smell* of food is inviting and it can also warn us of danger, although in solid fuel cookers, such as the Aga which I have at home, no smell escapes and it is easy to be caught out!

Touch a cake lightly to see that it is cooked through and *listen* to it singing – you will soon get to know when a particular recipe is ready. Test with a thin, warm skewer, and if any mixture sticks to the skewer, continue cooking. The exception to this is a fruit cake, which should still be slightly moist, never overcooked.

The size of eggs to be used is only given where accuracy is important. Otherwise, the size of eggs is not really crucial, although, generally, a larger egg gives just that bit of extra bulk and if a smaller one is used you may need to add milk to achieve the correct consistency for the recipe.

Although cooking times are always stated, ovens do vary; always check *before* the end of the cooking time, particularly the first time you make a recipe.

LINING CAKE TINS

It is important to line tins carefully and accurately, because creases can spoil the look of the baked cake. Inadequate lining can make a light cake difficult to turn out. Use greaseproof or parchment paper, and food cling film for microwave recipes.

Base-lining: Base-line tins by cutting out circles of greaseproof paper to fit your most popular tins, having these ready to use. Ready-cut circles of standard sizes are also available through specialist outlets. Use two circles in the base, unless the cake tins are non-stick in which case one is enough (Fig. 1). Lightly grease both the tins before lining, and the paper afterwards.

Line tins completely if there is a long cooking time or it is an exceptionally fragile mixture (Figs. 2 and 3).

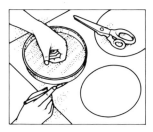
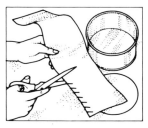
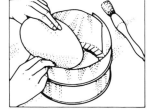
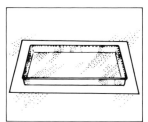
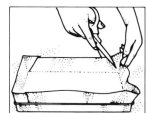

Fig. 1 *Base-lining;* Fig. 2 *Lining fully;* Fig. 3 *Lining a swiss roll tin*

Strip-line a loaf tin: Line loaf tins cutting a double piece of greaseproof paper (or when specified, aluminium foil) wide enough to fit the tin and long enough to protrude well over both ends (Figs. 6 and 7). Use these ends to help lift out the cake or dessert.

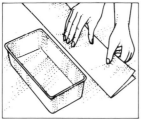 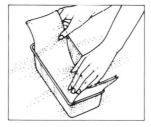

Fig. 6   Fig. 7

Allow cakes to cool in the tin for at least 5 minutes before attempting to turn them out, making sure they are not in a draught. Ease round the edge with a small palette knife, being careful not to cut into the cake, which happens all too often. Turn the cake out on to a wire cooling tray, carefully peel off the paper to allow the steam to escape, and then turn the cake the right way up (Figs. 8 and 9). Invest in two wire trays if you are a keen baker, because it is much easier to turn one on to the other. Ensure cakes are absolutely cold before storing, to let any steam escape.

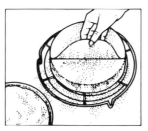 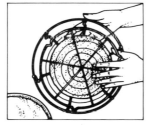

Fig. 8   Fig. 9

DECORATION

Piping: Greaseproof paper piping bags in several sizes are most useful (Fig. 10). Make these up in advance ready to use. Either cut off the tip and use, or cut off a slightly larger piece and pop in an icing pipe. When piping chocolate, it is easier not to use a metal pipe as it clogs up very quickly. When piping stars or rosettes on a cake or dessert, to add that professional finish, pipe rosettes at all four quarters and then fill in between them to ensure they are evenly spaced.

When grating the rind of citrus fruit, use a fine grater and only the coloured skin of the fruit, never the white pith. Grating the pith often makes the recipe bitter and spoils it.

Chocolate can be grated on various sizes of grater, or the 'Mouli' type is excellent for finely grated chocolate. Have the chocolate at room temperature, not too cold, for grating, chopping and making large curls with a vegetable peeler.

Cut Cadbury's Flake with a sharp knife either lengthways or into two or three across the Flake (Fig. 1, page 12). Use with the uncut side uppermost so that the cut edges do not show. Rub Cadbury's Buttons lightly between your fingers to make them shine when they are to be used for decoration.

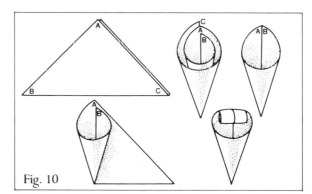

Fig. 10

Piquant Fudge Sauce

120 ml (6 tablespoons) golden syrup
250 g (9 oz) soft brown sugar
50 g (2 oz) butter
75 ml (3 fl oz) water
170 g (6 oz) can of evaporated milk
finely grated rind and juice of 1 small lemon

Measure the syrup with a hot metal spoon into a pan. Add the sugar, butter and water, and then heat gently, stirring occasionally, until the sugar has dissolved. Bring to the boil and then take off the heat. Stir in the evaporated milk, lemon rind and the strained juice.

Chocolate Fudge Sauce: Add 40 ml (a rounded tablespoon) of Cadbury's Bournville cocoa.

Honey Chocolate Sauce

100 g bar of Cadbury's Bournville chocolate
40 ml (2 tablespoons) honey
40 ml (2 tablespoons) lemon juice
50 g (2 oz) unsalted butter
20 ml (1 tablespoon) cornflour
125 ml (¼ pint) water

Break the chocolate into a pan, then stir with the other ingredients over a gentle heat until mixed together. Bring to the boil, stirring continuously, and boil for a minute. Serve immediately.

Speedy Chocolate Sauce

This is the sauce that I most usually make when in a hurry. It is excellent with pears and ice cream and can be re-heated and added to as you wish.

Blend more or less equal quantities, about 80 ml (2 rounded tablespoons), of Cadbury's Bournville cocoa, soft brown sugar and golden syrup together in a pan with 125 ml (¼ pint) pear or other canned syrup or fruit juice (or water). Stir slowly until boiling and then simmer for a couple of minutes. Pour into a jug. It keeps well, covered, in the fridge ready to use again.

For a malty flavour, add the same quantity of Cadbury's Bournvita with the cocoa. Additional flavours can be added at will and these quantities are easily increased, providing the proportions are kept correct.

Chocolate Fruit Sauce; Old-fashioned Upside-down Pudding (page 27)

Chocolate Fruit Sauce

25 g (1 oz) Cadbury's Bournville cocoa
20 ml (1 tablespoon) cornflour or custard powder
reserved fruit juice from a 411 g (14½ oz) can
40 ml (2 tablespoons) golden syrup
50 g (2 oz) butter
25 g (1 oz) sugar
125 ml (¼ pint) milk

In a pan, blend the cocoa and cornflour or custard powder with the fruit juice. Add the golden syrup, butter and sugar to taste and then heat slowly, stirring continuously, until the sauce thickens. Stir in the milk and heat again until just beginning to boil. Serve hot, with Old-fashioned Upside-down Pudding (page 27). This reheats well in the microwave.

Chocolate Custard

40 ml (2 tablespoons) cornflour or custard powder
40 ml (2 tablespoons) Cadbury's Bournville cocoa
25 g (1 oz) caster or soft brown sugar
juice from a 411 g (14¹/₂ oz) can of fruit
275 ml (¹/₂ pint) milk

Blend the cornflour or custard powder, cocoa and sugar with some of the fruit juice in a pan. When smooth, add the remaining juice and stir over a gentle heat as it thickens until boiling. Gradually stir in the milk and heat through but do not boil. Serve hot.

Serves about 6

Rich Chocolate Butter Cream

Known in French as *crème au beurre*, this can be an alternative to butter icing, chocolate and cream icings or frostings when you want a very special recipe. A pile of meringues sandwiched together with this makes an excellent party dessert, especially as it is better left for a day or two before eating. It is rather an effort, but delicious.

150 g Cadbury's Bournville chocolate
175 g (6 oz) unsalted butter
175 g (6 oz) granulated sugar
75 ml (3 fl oz) water
3 egg yolks

Break up the chocolate and leave to melt. Cream the butter until nice and soft, preferably with a mixer. Dissolve the sugar in the water over a very gentle heat, and when absolutely clear, boil rapidly to the short thread stage: you should be able to draw out a short, unbroken thread from the syrup off the end of a wooden spoon, between lightly oiled fingers. Make sure this stage is reached, otherwise the rich butter cream will not thicken enough.

Beat the egg yolks really hard using an electric mixer. Continue beating and slowly pour in the hot syrup as the mixture thickens and becomes very pale. Now beat in the soft butter, a spoonful at a time. Lastly, slowly add the melted chocolate, giving it a good final beating. Keep the butter cream in the refrigerator. Allow to soften before using.

Creamy Fudge Icing

100 g bar of Cadbury's Bournville chocolate
125 g (4 oz) butter
350 g (12 oz) icing sugar
40–60 ml (2–3 tablespoons) single cream or milk

Melt the chocolate with the butter in a basin over a pan of hot water. Sieve in the icing sugar and beat hard. Add the cream or milk, making a softish consistency. Leave to cool, and then beat again so that the icing is spreadable and ready to use.

Chocolate Fudge Icing

200 g bar of Cadbury's Bournville chocolate
1 small can of evaporated milk
225 g (8 oz) icing sugar, sieved

Break up the chocolate and melt it in a fairly large bowl over a pan of hot water. When completely melted, add the evaporated milk and beat together, still over the heat, so that the mixture is well mixed and starts to gain in bulk. Off the heat, cool the mixture a little before stirring in the sieved icing sugar. Place the icing in a refrigerator, or stand the bowl in ice-cold water, beating occasionally, until the icing becomes hard enough to spread over the cake.

Makes enough to cover a 20 cm (8-inch) cake

Royal Icing

450 g (1 lb) icing sugar
2 × size 2 egg whites
5 ml (1 teaspoon) lemon juice
5 ml (1 teaspoon) glycerine

Sieve the sugar into a bowl and then beat in the egg whites, and continue beating really hard until it is absolutely white. This is best done with an electric mixer. Beat in the lemon juice and glycerine, adjusting the consistency as you wish. It should be able to stand in stiff peaks and be snowy-white. Keep covered at all times; a damp cloth over the bowl or a sealed plastic container is good.

Should a softer consistency be required, for piping for example, slowly beat in more egg white or lemon juice, not water.

Chocolate Fondant

40 ml (2 tablespoons) liquid glucose
100 g bar of Cadbury's Bournville chocolate
1 × size 2 egg white
450 g (1 lb) icing sugar, sieved

Warm the glucose, then measure the amount into a bowl suspended over a pan of hot water. Add the broken-up chocolate and leave to melt. A microwave on DEFROST may also be used, for 3–4 minutes. Either cool the bowl or transfer the mixture to another bowl, adding the egg white and sieved icing sugar. Beat or knead the fondant until silky smooth, then keep airtight, well wrapped in a polythene bag, until required. Roll out on a surface lightly dusted with cocoa.

Makes enough to cover a 20–23 cm (8–9 inch) cake

Chocolate Butter Icing

It is easy to adapt this amount by increasing the ingredients, keeping the proportions correct. For a richer icing, use equal quantities of sugar to fat; for a family version, the icing sugar may be increased to double the quantity of butter used.

175 g (6 oz) slightly salted butter
250 g (9 oz) icing sugar
vanilla essence
25 g (1 oz) Cadbury's Bournville cocoa

Soften the butter but do not melt in the oven or it will be too soft. Cream the butter well in a bowl, preferably with an electric mixer. Sift in the icing sugar and a few drops of essence; beat really hard until the mixture has a good fluffy texture and is pale in colour. Mix the cocoa to a paste with a very little boiling water and when cool, beat it into the icing.

Flavourings: Fruit essences or finely grated rinds; coffee, peppermint and finely chopped nuts are all usual additions. Adding a little brandy instead of the vanilla makes a quick change, or use brandy essence.

Vanilla Butter Icing: To make vanilla butter icing, omit the cocoa.

Chocolate & Orange Mousse

A custard-based mousse which goes further than, but has a different texture to, the whisked egg versions.

200 g bar of Cadbury's Bournville chocolate
568 ml (1 pint) milk
1 orange
15 ml (3 teaspoons) gelatine
3 eggs, separated
25 g (1 oz) caster sugar
284 ml (½ pint) whipping cream
40 ml (2 tablespoons) brandy (optional)

a fairly large glass bowl, 1.4 litres (2½ pints)
  capacity
a piping bag with star pipe

Make some chocolate curls for the decoration (page 12) and reserve. Break up the remaining chocolate and melt it with the milk and finely grated orange rind (reserve a strip of rind to decorate), allowing the flavours to infuse. Dissolve the gelatine in the orange juice over a very gentle heat, or in a microwave on HIGH for 1 minute. Whisk the egg yolks and sugar together until paler in colour and then beat in the chocolate milk and gelatine. Whip the cream lightly and fold in, with the brandy, then the whisked egg whites. Pour into the dish and leave in the refrigerator overnight to set.

Decorate with the remaining cream piped into whirls, the chocolate curls and the strand of orange rind.

Serves 6–8

Chocolate Sandwich Cake; Chocolate & Orange Mousse; Kracolates

Kracolates

Made and loved by people of all ages, this must be one of the recipes most often made at home. No chocolate cookery book would be complete without it.

100 g bar of Cadbury's Bournville chocolate
50 g (2 oz) butter or margarine
20 ml (1 tablespoon) golden syrup
20 ml (1 tablespoon) Cadbury's drinking chocolate
125 g (4 oz) cornflakes or other cereal

about 15 paper cake cases

Break up the chocolate and melt it with the fat, syrup and drinking chocolate in a fairly large pan over a gentle heat, or in a bowl in a microwave on DEFROST for 2 minutes.

Stir until smooth, then stir in the cereals, using a mixture if you have some to use up. Coat well to cover completely in chocolate then spoon the mixture into the paper cases, arranged on a tray. Press the mixture together so that it will stick. Chill in a refrigerator.

Makes about 15

Chocolate Sandwich Cake

The most standard of cakes, but if you can make a light Victoria Sandwich cake, no other cake will defeat you!

175 g (6 oz) margarine or butter
175 g (6 oz) caster or soft brown sugar
3 × size 2 or 3 eggs
150 g (5 oz) self-raising flour
25 g (1 oz) Cadbury's Bournville cocoa

two 19 cm (7¹/₂-inch), round sandwich tins

Lightly grease the cake tins (a butter paper is ideal), line with two circles of greaseproof paper cut to fit, then grease the paper lining too.

Cream the fat and sugar together really well, using an electric mixer if available. This is easier if the fat is at room temperature, or if you warm the bowl and beater blades in the oven. The mixture should become lighter in colour and texture, and this applies whether white or brown sugar is used. Break the eggs separately then mix in, with a teaspoon of flour per egg. Mix in the remaining flour and cocoa, sieved together. Occasionally a little milk or warm water may be necessary to get the mixture to a softish dropping consistency.

Divide the mixture *equally* between the tins – it is worth weighing them if in doubt – smooth over the tops and hollow the centre a little. Bake side by side at Gas Mark 5/190°C/375°F for about 25 minutes, until cooked through yet springy to touch. Leave the cakes in the tins to cool a little before turning out carefully.

Peel off the paper lining and then turn the cakes the right way up. Ideally, two cooling trays are needed. Leave until absolutely cold before sandwiching together with butter icing or jam. Sprinkle the top with caster or icing sugar.

Serves 6–8

Chocolate Shortcrust Pastry

Chocolate flans make a welcome change.

100 g bar of Cadbury's Bournville chocolate
125 g (4 oz) butter or margarine
225 g (8 oz) plain flour

Break up the chocolate and melt it in a bowl over a pan of hot water; then cool. Rub the fat into the flour until the mixture resembles breadcrumbs. Add the cool chocolate and bind together with a very little cold water, about 20 ml (1 tablespoon). Work into a ball and wrap up and keep in the fridge to use as required within a few hours.

Roll out carefully, or alternatively, as the pastry is quite 'short', press it into the flan dish, being careful to avoid thick pastry in the corners. Prick the base and bake at Gas Mark 4/180°C/350°F for 20–25 minutes if to be used with a separate filling. Otherwise, use as the recipe directs.

Makes about 450 g (1 lb), or enough to line a 20–23 cm (8–9 inch) flan dish

Macaroon Cake

FOR THE CAKE
50 g (2 oz) softened butter
125 g (4 oz) light soft brown sugar
25 g (1 oz) self-raising flour
25 g (1 oz) wholemeal flour
2.5 ml (½ teaspoon) baking powder
50 g (2 oz) ground almonds
2 × size 2 eggs
a few drops of vanilla, rum or orange essence
4 Cadbury's Flake from the family box
TO COMPLETE
75 g (3 oz) softened butter
150 g (5 oz) icing sugar, sieved
finely grated rind of 1 orange
40 ml (2 tablespoons) natural yogurt
2–4 Cadbury's Flake from the family box

an 18 cm (7-inch) square cake tin, greased and base-lined

Beat together all the cake ingredients, except the Flake, for a good 3 minutes until thoroughly mixed. Mix in the crumbled Flake, then turn into the tin and smooth over the surface. Bake at Gas Mark 4/180°C/350°F for about 45 minutes until nicely browned and cooked through. Leave in the tin for 5 minutes before turning out to cool on a wire tray. Peel off the paper and turn the cake the right way up.

Prepare the icing by beating the softened butter with the icing sugar until much paler in colour. Beat in the orange rind and yogurt. Spread the top of the cake with icing; then crumble over the Flake, using as many as you wish. The icing may also be piped in diagonal lines, with the crumbled Flake in between for a smarter effect. Lift on to a plate or board.

Serves 8 generously

Chocolate Swiss Roll

Known as a fatless sponge mixture, this is easy to make once you have the knack. Nothing is nicer than a good home-made swiss roll, freshly made, perhaps filled with jam and whipped cream, or as we have here, with the surprise of Flake in the centre.

3 × size 2 eggs
75 g (3 oz) caster sugar
a few drops of vanilla essence
75 g (3 oz) plain flour
25 g (1 oz) Cadbury's Bournville cocoa
20 ml (1 tablespoon) warm water
TO COMPLETE
175 g (6 oz) Vanilla Butter Icing (page 20)
5 Cadbury's Flake from the family box

a 25 × 35 cm (10 × 14 inch) swiss roll tin
a piping bag with star pipe
greaseproof paper

Lightly grease the tin and line with greaseproof paper as illustrated in Fig. 3 on page 14.

The size of the eggs makes a difference to the size of the swiss roll, so use large, fresh eggs. Break them individually into a cup, then place in a mixer bowl, or in a bowl over a pan of hot but not boiling water. Measure in the sugar and essence, then whisk hard for about 10 minutes until a definite trail is left in the mixture. You should be able to write three initials and still see the first one in the mixture when the texture is correct. If in doubt, whisk again – it will not hurt.

Sieve the flour and cocoa together and then sieve into the eggs. Using a metal spoon or spatula, carefully fold in the dry ingredients, ensuring no dry pockets are left. Turn the mixture into the tin but do not spread.

Instead, tilt the tin and let the mixture find its own level. Bake in a fairly hot oven, Gas Mark 6/200°C/400°F, for about 12 minutes, until set firm yet springy to the touch. You should just hear the sponge 'singing'.

Have ready a large piece of greaseproof paper dusted with caster sugar. Gently turn the swiss roll on to this and peel off the paper lining, using a flat-bladed knife to press against it, helping to prevent the sponge coming away. Mark a dent in the sponge about 1 cm (½ inch) in at one short end, then carefully roll up the sponge, with the paper inside. Roll it as tightly as you conveniently can without breaking it. Leave to cool on a wire tray.

Meanwhile, prepare the butter icing to a spreadable consistency. Unroll the swiss roll carefully, spread with two-thirds of the butter icing, lay 2½ Flake end to end along the marked dent and roll up again tightly. Decorate the top with piped butter icing and halved Flake. Lift on to a plate and serve freshly made.

Tip: In our experience, it is a lack of whisking, or careless folding in of the flour, that is the main cause of heavy Swiss rolls, so take special care with these processes if you are inexperienced. To help avoid a failure in the beginning, cheat by adding 5 ml (1 level teaspoon) baking powder with the dry ingredients.

Serves 5–6

Genoese Sponge: to make a Genoese sponge, add 25 g (1 oz) melted warm, not hot, unsalted butter after the dry ingredients. This addition helps the sponge to keep better and is generally used for those small, iced, fancy cakes.

Macaroon Cake; Carnival Moments (page 27); Chocolate Swiss Roll

Mocha Chocolate Mousse

Make sure the egg whites are whisked really well, because the meringue consistency is the key to this mouthwatering mousse. Make and eat this on the same day.

100 g bar of Cadbury's Bournville chocolate
15 ml (3 teaspoons) dry instant coffee
4 egg whites
125 g (4 oz) caster sugar

4 individual glasses

Grate the chocolate and reserve some for the decoration. Melt the remaining chocolate with the coffee and 40 ml (2 tablespoons) water in a bowl over hot water (or substitute a coffee liqueur for the water), stirring occasionally. Whisk the egg whites stiffly, add half the sugar and whisk until as stiff again; fold in remaining sugar, then the chocolate mixture. Divide the mousse between the glasses, sprinkle with chocolate and then chill.

Serves 4

Puddle Pudding

The ever-popular chocolate sponge, with its own sauce underneath. This is a particularly nice version.

175 g (6 oz) self-raising flour
150 g (5 oz) caster or soft brown sugar
50 g (2 oz) Cadbury's Bournville cocoa
150 ml (6 fl oz) milk
10 ml (2 teaspoons) vanilla essence
50 g (2 oz) butter, melted
50 g (2 oz) soft brown sugar
550 ml (1 pint) hot water

a 1.4-litre (2½-pint), ovenproof dish, greased

Mix the flour and sugar with half the cocoa. Gradually beat in the milk, essence and melted butter and then pour into the prepared dish. Mix the remaining cocoa with the smaller amount of sugar and sprinkle over the top. Pour the water over the pudding and bake at Gas Mark 4/180°C/350°F for about 1 hour. The sponge should be crusty and cooked through, with a sauce underneath. Serve hot, with thin custard or single cream if liked.

Serves 8

Carnival Moments

125 g (4 oz) butter
50 g (2 oz) caster sugar
a few drops of vanilla or orange essence
125 g (4 oz) plain flour
25 g (1 oz) Cadbury's Bournville cocoa
100 g bar of Cadbury's Bournville chocolate
about 60 g (a good 2 oz) cornflakes, crushed lightly
6 glacé cherries

a baking tray, greased lightly

Cream the butter, sugar and essence well. Sieve in the flour and cocoa, add the chocolate, each square cut into four, mixing well until it binds together thoroughly. Divide the mixture in half, then each half into six. Roll these into balls and then roll each one in the lightly crushed cornflakes. Place them on the baking tray and flatten them slightly before baking them at Gas Mark 5/190°C/375°F for 12–15 minutes. Allow to harden a little before lifting off the tray to cool. Store in an airtight tin.

Makes 12   *Pictured on page 25*

Old-Fashioned Upside-Down Pudding

Although this pudding may look rather strange, it really is worth trying. A real family 'pud', for cold days. Use the reserved juice from the can of fruit to make Chocolate Fruit Sauce (page 17) to accompany this.

60 ml (3 tablespoons) apricot jam
411 g (14½ oz) can of apricots
175 g (6 oz) fresh white breadcrumbs
100 g bar of Cadbury's Bournville chocolate
5 ml (1 teaspoon) ground mixed spice
175 g (6 oz) margarine
175 g (6 oz) caster sugar
2 eggs
125 ml (¼ pint) milk

a 19 or 20 cm (7½- or 8-inch), ovenproof dish or
   fairly deep cake tin, greased

Spread the jam in the dish and then arrange seven apricots on top, cut-side upwards; reserve the juice to use in the sauce. Chop the remaining apricots. Grate the chocolate into the breadcrumbs and add the spice.

Cream the margarine and sugar together well, gradually beat in the eggs, the breadcrumb mixture and the milk (the mixture may look curdled at this stage). Fold in the chopped apricots and turn the mixture into the dish, being careful not to disturb the apricots in the base. Bake at Gas Mark 5/190°C/375°F for about 1 hour until nice and crisp on top and cooked through. Turn on to a warm plate and serve hot with the sauce.

Serves 6   *Pictured on page 17*

Beautifully Baked

Cakes, puddings and shortbreads are all here, with both plain and fancy recipes. The Chocolate Parkin and Spicy Chocolate Cake get better and better when they are kept; Crusty Surprise is a real family pudding to enjoy. Other recipes to dress up for those special occasions include Buttons and Bows Cake for a teatime celebration or this Tropical Temptation, an original hot trifle.

Tropical Temptation

A hot trifle with plenty of spice. Select more unusual fruit when you can, mixing fresh and canned quite freely.

225 g (8 oz) ginger cake, sliced
432 g (15½ oz) can of pineapple pieces in natural juice
40 ml (2 tablespoons) rum
2 oranges
2 bananas
2 kiwi fruit
FOR THE CHOCOLATE CUSTARD
60 ml (3 tablespoons) cornflour or custard powder
40 ml (2 tablespoons) caster sugar
2 egg yolks
568 ml (1 pint) milk
100 g bar of Cadbury's Bournville chocolate
FOR THE MERINGUE TOPPING
2 egg whites
125 g (4 oz) caster sugar
25 g (1 oz) flaked almonds

a 2.2-litre (4-pint) ovenproof dish

Place the slices of cake in the dish. Drain off the pineapple juice and then pour half of it, mixed with the rum, over the cake, allowing it to soak through. Prepare the fruit and mix the pineapple, segmented oranges, and sliced bananas and kiwi fruit together and put into the dish.

Make the custard by blending the cornflour, sugar and egg yolks into a paste with the remaining pineapple juice. Heat the milk, then stir the two together so that it thickens over a gentle heat. Break up the chocolate and melt into the custard. Cool slightly before pouring over the fruit.

To make the meringue, whisk the egg whites stiffly, add half the sugar and whisk until as stiff again; fold in the remaining sugar. Pile the meringue on the custard, covering it completely, then sprinkle with the flaked almonds. Bake at Gas Mark 4/180°C/350°F for 15–20 minutes so that the meringue looks attractive. Serve whilst still hot.

Serves 8 generously

Tropical Temptation; Kumquat Crunch (page 35)

Craggy Shortbread

150 g Cadbury's Bournville chocolate
225 g (8 oz) plain flour
5 ml (1 teaspoon) baking powder
2.5 ml (½ teaspoon) ground ginger
125 g (4 oz) butter
50 g (2 oz) soft brown sugar
25 g (1 oz) ground almonds
a little beaten egg
50 g (2 oz) stem ginger, chopped
8 Cadbury's Flake from the family box
a few flaked almonds

a 20 cm (8-inch), loose-based, round cake tin,
   greased lightly

Melt the chocolate. Sieve the dry ingredients together, rub in the butter and then work in the sugar, ground almonds and melted chocolate. Knead lightly together and then press half the mixture into the tin. Brush with egg and sprinkle with the chopped ginger and four crushed Flake. Press the remaining mixture on top. Brush with egg again before sprinkling with the almonds and the remaining roughly crushed Flake. Mark into eight or ten even wedges. Bake in a slow oven, Gas Mark 2/150°C/300°F, for 30–40 minutes until cooked through. Cut into the wedges. The shortbread may be dusted with icing sugar when cold.

Serves 8–10

Rocky Ramblers

FOR THE BASE
125 g (4 oz) margarine
25 g (1 oz) Cadbury's Bournville cocoa
150 g (5 oz) self-raising flour
225 g (8 oz) soft brown sugar
75 g (3 oz) walnuts, chopped
5 ml (1 teaspoon) vanilla essence
2 eggs
FOR THE TOPPING
175 g (6 oz) cream cheese
75 g (3 oz) caster sugar
40 ml (2 tablespoons) self-raising flour
50 g (2 oz) margarine
1 egg
2.5 ml (½ teaspoon) vanilla essence
100 g bar of Bournville plain chocolate, grated

an 18 × 28 cm (7 × 11 inch) shallow cake tin,
   greased and floured

For the base, in a fairly large saucepan, melt the margarine with the cocoa. Off the heat, stir in the flour, sugar, nuts, essence and the eggs. When well mixed, spread the mixture in the tin.

For the topping, beat the cream cheese with the sugar, flour, margarine, egg and essence until smooth and almost white in colour. Spread this carefully over the base. Sprinkle grated chocolate on top, then bake at Gas Mark 4/180°C/350°F for 45–55 minutes, until risen and cooked through. Cool in the tin; it will sink in the middle. Cut into bars. Lift out carefully.

Makes 16

Hideaway Cake

125 g (4 oz) butter
125 g (4 oz) caster or soft brown sugar
2 eggs, beaten
125 g (4 oz) plain flour
60 g (a good 2 oz) Cadbury's drinking chocolate
5 ml (1 level teaspoon) baking powder
50 g (2 oz) chopped walnuts
10 ml (2 teaspoons) coffee essence or instant coffee mixed with a little hot water
100 g bar of Cadbury's Dairy Milk milk chocolate

a 19 cm (7½-inch) sandwich tin at least 4.5 cm (1½ inches) deep, greased and base-lined

Cream the butter and sugar together. Beat the eggs in gradually. Sieve the dry ingredients together and fold them in, with the nuts and liquid coffee or coffee essence. (This can be done in a food processor.)

Chop each square of chocolate into four (it is worth doing this by hand) and then fold in. Turn the mixture into the tin, hollowing out the centre slightly. Bake at Gas Mark 4/180°C/350°F for 50 minutes. Leave to cool a little in the tin before turning out. Dust with sugar or spread the top with chocolate.

Note: This cake freezes well but is especially good served on the day it is baked.   *Serves about 8*

Craggy Shortbread; Rocky Ramblers

Flake Woodland

A cake with some fruit in it for Christmas time, yet not too rich. It is worthy of being a table decoration in itself. Get the children to help put the thin pieces of Flake in position.

FOR THE CAKE
175 g (6 oz) soft margarine
175 g (6 oz) soft brown sugar
3 eggs, beaten
175 g (6 oz) self-raising flour
50 g (2 oz) ground almonds
60 ml (3 tablespoons) mincemeat
100 g bar of Cadbury's Bournville chocolate
FOR THE ICING AND DECORATION
100 g bar of Cadbury's Bournville chocolate
75 g (3 oz) granulated sugar
2 egg yolks
175 g (6 oz) unsalted butter, softened at room temperature
a Cadbury's Flake family box
a packet of Cadbury's milk chocolate Buttons
red sugar balls

an 18 cm (7-inch), round cake tin, greased and base-lined
a baking tray
a 23 cm (9-inch), round cake board
greaseproof or baking parchment
a greaseproof paper piping bag

For the cake, cream the margarine and sugar together, and then gradually add the beaten eggs. Fold in the flour, with the ground almonds and mincemeat. Cut each square of chocolate into four and add to the mixture, beating well. Turn the mixture into the tin and place on the baking tray, with an ovenproof wedge under one side of the tin so that the cake is baked at an angle. The wedge should be no deeper than 2 cm (½ inch); a scale weight is ideal. Bake at Gas Mark 4/180°C/350°F for 1¼–1½ hours, until cooked through. Turn out and cool.

Make the icing by melting half the chocolate in a pan with 20 ml (1 tablespoon) of water. Dissolve the sugar in 80 ml (4 tablespoons) of water until quite clear, and then boil rapidly for about 2 minutes, until it forms a thin syrup. Whisk the egg yolks and melted chocolate together and gradually pour on the syrup, whisking continuously, until cooled and thickened, Gradually beat in the softened butter a little at a time. Leave until quite cold.

Place the cake on the cake board. Cover it completely with the icing, and then mark the top into concentric rings with a fork to look like the top of a log. Cut about ten of the Flakes into thin pieces. Carefully press these on to the side of the cake, mixing up the larger and smaller pieces, to resemble the bark of a tree.

Melt the remaining chocolate in a bowl over hot water. Use it to pipe ivy-leaf shapes in several sizes (see page 12). Leave in a cool place to set.

Cut two Flake into short pieces and with the Buttons, make small mushrooms, sticking the Buttons on with a little melted chocolate. Dust lightly with icing sugar. Decorate the top of the cake with clumps of these mushrooms and sprays of ivy leaves, dotting a few red sugar 'berries' around.

Tip: Try to have uncut edges of Flake round the top.

Serves 8 or more

Flake Woodland

Spicy Chocolate Cake

A moist plain cake with an unusual texture. The black treacle blends admirably with the chocolate and spice.

100 g bar of Cadbury's Bournville chocolate
125 g (4 oz) slightly salted butter
125 g (4 oz) dark soft brown sugar
20 ml (1 tablespoon) black treacle
3 eggs
50 g (2 oz) self-raising flour
5 ml (1 teaspoon) ground mixed spice
75 g (3 oz) ground almonds
75 g (3 oz) fresh breadcrumbs
100 ml (5 tablespoons) lemon curd or a fruit conserve
    (optional)

a 19 cm (7½-inch), round cake tin, greased and
    base-lined

Melt the chocolate. Cream the butter, sugar and treacle together really well until the mixture becomes paler, then beat in the eggs with a spoonful of flour per egg. Add the remaining flour, the spice and ground almonds, and then the breadcrumbs. Finally stir in the chocolate and turn the mixture into the tin, hollowing out the centre slightly. Bake at Gas Mark 4/180°C/350°F for 45–50 minutes, until set but still moist. It does not matter if it is a bit soft in the middle. Leave in the tin to cool.

Loosen the cake round the edge, then turn out. Slice the cake through the centre and sandwich it together with the lemon curd or conserve. You can also leave this plain, or put a lemon glacé icing on top.

Tip: This cake makes a good accompaniment to the Banana Creole (page 64), which is the way we first tried it.   *Serves 6–8*

Button Bakes

20 ml (1 tablespoon) cornflour
50 g (2 oz) caster sugar
3 × size 2 eggs, separated
275 ml (½ pint) milk
a knob of butter
5 ml (1 teaspoon) vanilla essence
a packet of Cadbury's milk chocolate Buttons
icing sugar, to dust

6 individual ramekin dishes
a baking tray

Stir the cornflour, sugar and egg yolks together. Heat the milk and then pour it into the egg mixture; return to the pan and heat gently, stirring continuously, until the custard thickens. Off the heat, stir in the butter and essence, and then allow to cool. This can be done well in advance.

Whisk the egg whites stiffly, fold one spoonful of the custard mixture into the egg whites, then fold them back into the custard with a cut and fold action to avoid knocking out the air. Quickly stir in the Buttons (a few more will not hurt), divide the mixture between the dishes and lift on to a baking tray. Bake in a very hot oven at Gas Mark 8/230°C/450°F for 12–15 minutes until they are well risen and golden brown. Dredge with icing sugar and serve immediately.

Tip: Folding a little of the stiffer mixture into whisked egg whites, before folding them all in, helps to incorporate the two mixtures better.

Note: These little puddings should be eaten straight from the oven as they tend to sink quickly, but even then, the flavour is delicious.

Makes 6

Kumquat Crunch

A rather unusual recipe in which leftover toast can be used. Do use white bread here, because brown makes the mixture too heavy.

FOR THE BASE
225 g (8 oz) kumquats
125 ml (¼ pint) orange juice
40 ml (2 tablespoons) brandy
125 g (4 oz) white toast, crusts removed
125 g (4 oz) digestive biscuits
75 g (3 oz) plain flour
50 g (2 oz) ground almonds
50 g (2 oz) caster sugar
50 g (2 oz) Cadbury's drinking chocolate
200 g (7 oz) butter
TO COMPLETE
284 ml (½ pint) double cream
150 g (5 oz) carton of thick and creamy apricot and mango yogurt

a 23 cm (9-inch) flan ring on a baking tray
a piping bag with a star pipe

Place the kumquats, orange juice and brandy in a saucepan and slowly bring to the boil; simmer until all the liquid has disappeared. Leave to cool.

Break the toast and biscuits into a food processor (or liquidiser) and process until quite fine. Add the flour, ground almonds, sugar and drinking chocolate, with the butter cut into small pieces, then process until the mixture resembles coarse breadcrumbs. (This will have to be done by hand if a liquidiser is used.) Press half the mixture into the flan ring and smooth over the surface. Bake at Gas Mark 3/170°C/325°F for 25 minutes. Cool briefly, before lifting off the ring. Make the second layer in the same way, using a second baking tray if available. Cool, then store in an air-tight container until required.

Place one layer on a flat plate. Whip the cream and yogurt together until the mixture holds its shape. Using half, pipe a pattern of cream on the top layer. Spread all the remaining cream on the base layer. Reserve about eight nice pieces of fruit, chop the remainder and spread over the cream. Lift on the top layer and complete the decoration with the fruit.

Note: Kumquats are seasonal, but you can substitute 450 g (1 lb) apricots or use a can, draining off the syrup.

Serves 8   *Pictured on page 29*

Shortcake Ring

Although this is specially suitable for Christmas time, do try it on other occasions.

FOR THE SHORTCAKE
200 g (7 oz) plain flour
25 g (1 oz) semolina or rice flour
40 ml (2 tablespoons) Cadbury's Bournville cocoa
40 ml (2 tablespoons) soft brown sugar
150 g (5 oz) butter
TO COMPLETE
100 g bar of Cadbury's Bournville chocolate
40 ml (2 tablespoons) apricot jam
50 g (2 oz) each of candied pineapple, mixed peel, glacé cherries, stoned dates, and walnuts or blanched almonds
a little angelica
25 g (1 oz) icing sugar
lemon juice

a baking tray

Measure the dry ingredients and sugar for the short-cake into a bowl. Rub in the butter until the mixture resembles breadcrumbs (this can be done in a food processor). Work the mixture together. Roll on a lightly floured surface into a 25 cm (10-inch) circle. Lift this on to the baking tray. Cut out a 10 cm (4-inch) circle from the centre and use this to make a few diamond-shaped pastry leaves, marking on the veins; place on the baking tray too. Prick the ring with a fork and crimp the edge. Allow to rest in the fridge for ½ hour if possible, then bake at Gas Mark 5/ 190°C/375°F for about 12 minutes until cooked.

Chop each square of chocolate into four and sprinkle them over the shortcake immediately it comes out of the oven. Warm the jam and stir in all the fruit and the nuts, chopped as necessary. Carefully spread this over the cool shortcake ring; add the biscuit and angelica leaves. Mix the icing sugar with lemon juice, then drizzle the glacé icing over the top. Lift on to a pretty plate or cake board and decorate with a ribbon bow.

Serves about 8

Shortcake Ring; Chocolate Parkin; Crusted Loaf Cake

Chocolate Parkin

250 g (9 oz) plain flour
12.5 ml (2½ teaspoons) ground ginger
12.5 ml (2½ teaspoons) baking powder
2.5 ml (½ teaspoon) bicarbonate of soda
50 g (2 oz) Cadbury's Bournville cocoa
175 g (6 oz) margarine
175 g (6 oz) soft brown sugar
350 g (12 oz) golden syrup
275 ml (½ pint) milk
1 egg, beaten
175 g (6 oz) medium oatmeal
100 g bar of Cadbury's Bournville chocolate, chopped

a 23 cm (9-inch) square, deep cake tin or a roasting
  tin, greased and base-lined

Sieve all the dry ingredients together. Melt the margarine, sugar and syrup in a fairly large pan and stir over a gentle heat until the sugar has dissolved. Stir in the milk and egg, then the oatmeal, the dry ingredients and the chopped chocolate, making sure it is well mixed. Pour into the tin and bake at Gas Mark 4/180°C/350°F for 1–1¼ hours, until cooked but not overcooked. It doesn't matter if this type of recipe is a bit soggy, but it should not be runny in the centre. Leave to cool in the tin and then turn out. Serve on its own or spread with butter.

Note: This improves if kept tightly wrapped for two days.

Serves 8 or more

Crusted Loaf Cake

FOR THE CAKE
125 g (4 oz) soft margarine
175 g (6 oz) caster sugar
2 eggs
50 g (2 oz) desiccated coconut
80 ml (4 tablespoons) lime cordial
150 g (5 oz) self-raising flour
25 g (1 oz) Cadbury's Bournville cocoa
FOR THE SYRUP
75 g (3 oz) caster sugar
80 ml (4 tablespoons) lime cordial

a 1 kg (2 lb) loaf tin, greased and strip-lined

To make the cake, cream the margarine and sugar together, and gradually beat in the eggs. Beat in the coconut and cordial; fold in the flour and cocoa. Spoon the mixture into the tin, making the surface level, then bake at Gas Mark 4/180°C/350°F for about 55 minutes. Test with a skewer to see that it is cooked. Carefully lift out with the paper and cool. Clean the tin.

For the syrup, dissolve the sugar in the cordial over a gentle heat and when dissolved and clear, bring to the boil for 2 or 3 minutes till it forms a thin syrup. Return the cake to the tin and pour over the syrup, poking it in with a skewer. Cool the cake in the tin. Spread slices with fruit curd or other spread if wished.

Serves 6

Crusty Surprise

The lovely spicy 'streusal' topping makes this a favourite family pudding. Don't leave out the cinnamon.

FOR THE SPONGE
125 g (4 oz) margarine
125 g (4 oz) caster or soft brown sugar
2 eggs
40 ml (2 tablespoons) milk
vanilla essence
25 ml (1 good tablespoon) Cadbury's Bournville cocoa
125 g (4 oz) self-raising flour
100 g bar of Cadbury's Dairy Milk milk chocolate, chopped
425 g (15 oz) can of pear halves
FOR THE TOPPING
50 g (2 oz) butter
50 g (2 oz) soft brown sugar
50 g (2 oz) self-raising flour
5 ml (1 teaspoon) ground cinnamon
FOR THE SAUCE
100 ml (4 fl oz) milk
1 egg yolk
40 ml (2 tablespoons) cornflour
20 ml (1 tablespoon) sugar
5 ml (1 teaspoon) vanilla or rum essence or finely grated rind of 1 small orange or a few drops of orange essence

a 20 cm (8-inch), round, loose-based tin or a similar sized ovenproof dish, greased lightly

For the cake, cream the margarine and sugar; gradually beat in the eggs, milk and a few drops of essence. Fold in the sieved cocoa and flour, with the chopped chocolate. Spread half the mixture evenly in the tin. Drain the pears, reserving the juice, and then arrange them in a circle on top, reserving one piece. Spread the remaining cake mixture over the fruit. Bake at Gas Mark 4/180°C/350°F for 45 minutes.

Meanwhile, make the topping by rubbing the butter into the sugar, flour and ground cinnamon. Sprinkle this over the base and return to the oven for a further ½ hour.

To make the sauce, blend the milk into the egg yolk, cornflour and sugar in a saucepan, and, when smooth, heat gently until thickened. Gradually stir in the reserved pear juice, whisking continuously until the mixture thickens and is heated through. Now add the flavouring of your choice.

Ease the pudding out of the tin on to a warm plate (if made in the dish, leave it). Decorate with slices of the reserved pear. Serve with the sauce.

Microwave tip: The pudding can be re-heated on HIGH for 2–3 minutes. The sauce can also be re-heated for 2–3 minutes in the jug.

Serves 7–8

Buttons & Bows Cake

A pretty cake that will adapt to many occasions. The fondant helps to keep the cake moist so that it stores well, for 1–2 weeks.

FOR THE CAKE
150 g (5 oz) self-raising flour
50 g (2 oz) Cadbury's Bournville cocoa
2.5 ml (½ teaspoon) bicarbonate of soda
125 g (4 oz) soft margarine
225 g (8 oz) dark soft brown sugar
2 eggs
25 g (1 oz) ground almonds
142 ml (¼ pint) soured cream
FOR THE FILLING AND DECORATION
80 ml (4 tablespoons) Grand Marnier or orange juice
60 ml (3 tablespoons) jelly marmalade
225 g (8 oz) marzipan
1 amount Chocolate Fondant (page 19)
a little Cadbury's Bournville cocoa
50 g bar of Cadbury's Bournville chocolate, melted
a packet each of Cadbury's milk chocolate and creamy-white Buttons

two 19 cm (7½-inch), sandwich tins, greased and base-lined
a 25 cm (10-inch) cake board or plate
a pastry wheel (optional)
a small greaseproof paper piping bag

Make the cake by placing all the ingredients in a mixing bowl and beating hard, preferably with an electric mixer, for a good 4 minutes until thoroughly blended. Divide the mixture equally between the tins then bake at Gas Mark 5/190°C/375°F for 30–35 minutes, until well risen and cooked. Turn out to cool.

Soak the sponges with 60 ml (3 tablespoons) liqueur or juice. Warm the remaining liquid with the marmalade and brush the cake bases. Roll 75 g (3 oz) marzipan to a circle the same size as the cakes and then sandwich back together with the marzipan in the centre; brush all over with marmalade.

Prepare the fondant. Dust the work surface with a little cocoa, then roll out the fondant large enough to cover the cake. Carefully smooth it over the cake and trim the edge. Lift on to the cake board.

Roll the remaining marzipan into a rectangle measuring the full width of the cake, about 28 cm (11 inches). With the pastry wheel, if using, or a knife, cut five 2.5 cm (1-inch) widthways strips and dampen the undersides slightly. Place two strips at right angles to each other over the cake (Fig. 1). Cut a 'V' at both ends of two more strips making them slightly shorter. Lay these at right angles to each other in between the first two (Fig. 2). Bend the two ends of the remaining strip to meet in the middle and pinch together lightly to make a bow (Fig. 3). Put a strip across the middle, made from re-rolled scraps; dampen slightly to secure. Place tissue paper inside the loops to support the marzipan until it hardens slightly (Fig. 4). Place the bow in the centre of the cake. Pipe small dots of chocolate on the marzipan ribbon whilst on the cake, then stick the Buttons on with melted chocolate to complete.
Serves about 12

Buttons & Bows Cake

Fig. 1

Fig. 2

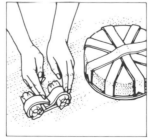

Fig. 3

Fig. 4

Classic Collection

Here we find many of the classic chocolate recipes which are hard to beat in taste terms. Try the American Fudge Cake topped with ice cream or even a Mississippi Mud Pie, rich and glorious. There are Refrigerator Cookies ready to whip out at a moment's notice, the universally popular No-Bake Biscuit Slice and Topping Brownies, light as air Flaky Éclairs or a Rich Chocolate Mousse, so browse through and make your choice.

Sachertorte

The ultimate in simplicity but perhaps the most famous of all chocolate cakes.

FOR THE CAKE
100 g bar of Cadbury's Bournville chocolate
125 g (4 oz) slightly salted butter
125 g (4 oz) caster sugar
6 × size 2 eggs, separated
125 g (4 oz) plain flour, sieved
60–80 ml (3–4 tablespoons) apricot jam
FOR THE ICING
200 g bar of Cadbury's Bournville chocolate
142 ml (¼ pint) double cream
125 g (4 oz) icing sugar, sieved

a 20 cm (8-inch), deep cake tin, greased and
*   base-lined*
a baking tray
a greaseproof paper piping bag

For the cake, melt the chocolate, then allow it to cool. Cream the butter and three-quarters of the sugar really well together, then beat in the egg yolks and melted chocolate. Fold in the sieved flour. Whisk the egg whites until they form peaks, fold in the remaining sugar and whisk again. Stir a little egg white into the mixture before folding in the remainder; turn into the tin. Place on a baking tray and bake at Gas Mark 4/ 180°C/350°F for 1–1¼ hours, until cooked. Leave for a few minutes before turning out to cool.

Cut the cake through the centre and sandwich together with apricot jam.

For the icing, melt the chocolate in a bowl over hot water, and then put a little in the piping bag and cool the remainder. Whisk in the cream and sieved icing sugar and then leave to cool and thicken enough to coat the back of a wooden spoon. Pour the icing over the cake on the wire tray, or spread it with a palette knife if preferred. Leave to set before piping a name in the centre, warming the chocolate in the bag in the oven or over hot water, to melt it again. Lift the cake on to a plate or board. This is often served just with whipped cream.

Serves 8

Sachertorte; Chocolate Roulade

Chocolate Roulade

Rich and wonderful, oozing with orange-flavoured cream, this classic dessert is really one for special occasions.

FOR THE SPONGE
100 g bar of Cadbury's Bournville chocolate
4 × size 2 eggs, separated
125 g (4 oz) caster sugar
FOR THE FILLING
284 ml (½ pint) double cream
150 g (5 oz) natural yogurt
2 oranges
20–40 ml (1–2 tablespoons) Grand Marnier
25 g (1 oz) flaked almonds, browned
5 Cadbury's Flake from the family box
FOR THE ICING
100 g bar of Cadbury's Bournville chocolate
5 ml (1 teaspoon) bland salad oil
40 g (1½ oz) icing sugar
20 ml (1 tablespoon) Grand Marnier

a 23 × 33 cm (9 × 13 inch) swiss roll tin, greased
   and lined
greaseproof paper
a piping bag fitted with a star pipe

To make the sponge, melt the chocolate with 10 ml (2 teaspoons) water in a bowl over a pan of hot water. Whisk the egg yolks and sugar together, preferably with an electric beater, until very pale in colour. Beat in the melted chocolate. Fold in the stiffly whisked egg whites, pour the mixture into the tin and level the surface by tilting the tin, not by spreading the mixture. Bake at Gas Mark 4/180°C/350°F for 20–25 minutes until cooked yet springy to touch. Cover with a clean, damp tea towel and leave to stand for at least 4 hours or overnight. This is important because otherwise the sponge will not roll up.

For the filling, whip the cream and yogurt together until the mixture holds its shape. Spoon two good spoonsful into the piping bag for the decoration. Add the finely grated rind of one orange to the remaining cream. Turn the roulade on to the greaseproof paper, peel off the paper lining and sprinkle with the liqueur. Spread the cream over the sponge but do not take it right to the edge as it will spread further when you roll up the sponge.

Segment the oranges and chop all but five segments, then place on the cream. Scatter with the nuts and two crumbled Flake. Roll up the roulade, using the paper to support it as you do so, then wrap the paper round as lightly as possible, lift on to a tray and refrigerate for about an hour to allow the cake mixture to become firm enough to handle without cracking.

For the icing, break the chocolate into a small pan with the oil and 40 ml (2 tablespoons) water and stir over a gentle heat until melted. Sieve in the icing sugar, add the liqueur and stir until smooth. Cool before spooning over the roulade. Lift on to a plate to serve.

Decorate with whirls of cream, the reserved orange segments and the reserved Flake, cut. Roulades are better eaten on the same day.

Tip: Vary the flavour of the filling as you wish: most of the well known combinations are suitable; try a coffee, mint or even a chocolate filling.

Serves 6–8

Mississippi Mud Pie

FOR THE PASTRY BASE
175 g (6 oz) butter, softened
75 g (3 oz) caster sugar
215 g (7½ oz) plain flour
40 g (1½ oz) cornflour
FOR THE FILLING
200 g bar of Cadbury's Bournville chocolate
125 g (4 oz) butter
20 ml (1 tablespoon) instant coffee, dissolved in
 20 ml (1 tablespoon) boiling water
142 ml (¼ pint) single cream
175 g (6 oz) dark soft brown sugar
3 eggs

a 23 cm (9-inch), deep, fluted flan tin or dish

For the base, cream the butter and sugar together thoroughly. Add both flours, making a fairly stiff dough. Press this into the flan tin as evenly as possible. Bake at Gas Mark 5/190°C/375°F for 15 minutes, until nicely browned.

For the filling, break up the chocolate and melt it in a pan with the butter and coffee. Off the heat, beat in the cream, sugar and eggs, and then pour the filling into the base. Bake for a further 30–40 minutes until the filling is set. Cool before serving, traditionally with whipped cream or ice cream.

Tip: Use Muscovado sugar in the filling if you have it, for an even richer flavour.

Serves 8

Refrigerator Cookies

Keep a roll of this mixture in the freezer ready for use.

125 g (4 oz) margarine
175 g (6 oz) caster sugar
1 egg
200 g (7 oz) self-raising flour
25 g (1 oz) Cadbury's Bournville cocoa
50 g (2 oz) walnuts, chopped
a Cadbury's Dairy Milk milk chocolate chunky bar
50 g (2 oz) glacé cherries, chopped
a few drops of vanilla essence

greaseproof paper
2 or 3 baking trays, greased lightly

Cream the fat and sugar together, and then add the egg and the sieved dry ingredients. Stir in the walnuts, the chocolate (each chunk cut into four or six), the chopped cherries and the essence, making a fairly soft dough. Form into a roll about 4 cm (1½ inches) in diameter and then wrap in a double layer of grease-proof paper. Wrap tightly again in foil and leave to harden, or freeze at this stage for up to a month.

Slice the roll into about 30 pieces and lay these on the baking trays, allowing room to spread. Bake in batches at Gas Mark 4/180°C/350°F for 15–20 minutes (or a little more if cooked from frozen). Cool a little before lifting off the trays.

Makes about 30   *Pictured on the back cover*

Grasshopper Pie

Pies are traditional in America. The short pastry contrasts well with the airy filling and is topped by a rich chocolate icing, to make this a classic of its kind.

1 amount of Chocolate Shortcrust Pastry (page 23)
FOR THE FILLING
15 ml (3 teaspoons) gelatine
225 g (8 oz) fromage frais
50 g (2 oz) caster sugar
80 ml (4 tablespoons) Crème de Menthe
2 egg whites
142 ml (¼ pint) double cream
FOR THE ICING
100 g bar of Cadbury's Bournville chocolate
40 ml (2 tablespoons) Cadbury's Bournville cocoa
50 g (2 oz) caster sugar
5 ml (1 teaspoon) bland salad oil
60 ml (3 tablespoons) water

a 25 cm (10-inch), loose-based flan tin

Make up the pastry as described, and then press it into the tin, using the back of a spoon to press it in evenly. Prick the base and bake at Gas Mark 4/180°C/350°F for 20–25 minutes, until cooked.

For the filling, sprinkle the gelatine on to 80 ml (4 tablespoons) of almost boiling water and stir until dissolved; allow to cool. Mix the fromage frais, sugar and liqueur together. Whisk the egg whites until they are peaking nicely and then whip the cream. Whisk the cold gelatine quickly into the fromage frais mixture. Whisk in the cream. Fold in the egg whites nice and evenly. Pour the filling into the pastry case and chill for several hours until set.

Place all the icing ingredients in a small pan and

melt over a low heat, stirring occasionally. When quite smooth, cool the icing and then neatly pour it over the pie filling. Leave until thickened and set a bit before serving, but it will not harden. Ease the pie out of the tin and serve with whipped cream if you like.

Tip: To make a chocolate filling, melt a 100 g bar of Cadbury's Bournville chocolate and substitute it for the Crème de Menthe, or have both in a Chocolate and Mint pie.

The pie can also be covered with large curls of chocolate, if you prefer.

Serves 8

Mississippi Mud Pie; Grasshopper Pie

Battenburg Cake

Always a popular cake, the marzipan helps keep it moist and succulent. Have a go at making it at home, it really isn't too difficult.

FOR THE CAKE
125 g (4 oz) soft margarine
125 g (4 oz) caster sugar
2 eggs
40 ml (2 tablespoons) milk
125 g (4 oz) self-raising flour
50 g (2 oz) ground almonds
2.5 ml (1/2 teaspoon) almond essence
20 ml (1 tablespoon) Cadbury's Bournville cocoa
TO COMPLETE
about 80 ml (4 tablespoons) apricot jam, melted
350 g (12 oz) marzipan
10 ml (2 tablespoons) Cadbury's Bournville cocoa

*a 19 cm (7 1/2-inch) square cake tin, greased and
    base-lined*

Divide the cake tin in half with a piece of cardboard that you have cut to fit and covered in foil.

For the cake, cream the margarine and sugar well together. Gradually beat in the eggs, with half the milk, and then fold in the flour and the ground almonds. Divide the mixture in half. Add the essence and 5 ml (1 teaspoon) of milk to one amount; add the cocoa with the small amount of milk remaining to the other. Stir in evenly, and then spread the mixtures, one either side of the board, in the tin, levelling the top. Bake at Gas Mark 5/190°C/375°F for about 1/2 hour, until risen and cooked through. Carefully turn out both oblong cakes and let them cool.

To assemble in the traditional shape, cut the cakes in half lengthways and then sandwich the different colours alternately together with the jam. Keep 75 g (3 oz) of the marzipan plain, and evenly knead the cocoa into the remainder. Reserve a further 75 g (3 oz) of the chocolate marzipan with the plain. Brush the assembled cake with jam. Roll the bigger piece of chocolate marzipan into a large enough oblong to cover all the long sides of the cake in one go. Wrap it round the cake, with the join underneath. Trim the edges and make sure the cake is square.

Mark the top with lines in a diamond pattern. Roll the two reserved pieces of marzipan into strips long enough to go down the sides and along the top of the cake, and a bit extra, so that they can be twisted together. Brush the edges with a little jam and press the strips into position. Lift on to a plate or board.

Serves 6–8

American Fudge Cake

This recipe is also known as 'Death by Chocolate', if it is topped with chocolate ice cream and lashings of whipped cream.

FOR THE CAKE
125 g (4 oz) butter
225 g (8 oz) dark soft brown sugar
2 eggs
142 ml (¼ pint) soured cream
175 g (6 oz) plain flour
5 ml (1 teaspoon) baking powder
2.5 ml (½ teaspoon) bicarbonate of soda
50 g (2 oz) Cadbury's Bournville cocoa
FOR THE FILLING
40 ml (2 tablespoons) Cadbury's Bournville cocoa
125 g (4 oz) butter
150 g (5 oz) icing sugar, sieved
vanilla essence
FOR THE FROSTING
200 g bar of Cadbury's Bournville chocolate
40 ml (2 tablespoons) Cadbury's Bournville cocoa
142 ml (¼ pint) double cream

two 20 cm (8-inch), shallow cake tins, greased and base-lined

For the cake, cream together the butter and sugar until the mixture is light in colour and texture. Gradually beat in the eggs, and then the soured cream (the mixture looks curdled at this stage). Sieve together the dry ingredients and fold them into the mixture. Divide the mixture equally between the tins. Bake at Gas Mark 5/190°C/375°F for 30–35 minutes, until cooked. Turn out on to a wire tray to cool.

Make the filling by mixing the cocoa with 40 ml (2 tablespoons) of boiling water to a smooth paste; allow to cool. Beat together the butter, sieved icing sugar and essence, until light and fluffy. Beat in the cocoa. Slice the cake in half and then sandwich the halves together with the filling.

For the frosting, melt the chocolate carefully. Make the cocoa into a paste with water as before and mix with the chocolate. Slowly whisk the cream into the chocolate until smooth and thickened. Spread the frosting evenly over the cake with a palette knife.

Serve in slices, with whipped cream or ice-cream. If possible warm each slice in a microwave or oven, if you have made the cake in advance: it can also be served cold but is definitely more interesting hot, with the contrast of ice cream.

Serves 8

Deep South Muffins; Battenburg Cake; American Fudge Cake

Deep South Muffins

Delicious served straight from the oven, with butter, maple syrup, honey or chocolate spread.

25 g (1 oz) bran
50 g (2 oz) raisins
275 ml (½ pint) milk
50 g (2 oz) margarine
150 g (5 oz) dark soft brown sugar
1 egg
150 g (5 oz) plain flour
25 g (1 oz) Cadbury's Bournville cocoa
15 ml (3 teaspoons) baking powder
100 g bar of Cadbury's Bournville chocolate

deep bun tins, well greased and floured

Combine the bran, raisins and milk in a bowl; leave to stand for 10 minutes. Cream the margarine and sugar, and then beat the egg into this runny mixture. Fold in the sieved dry ingredients, the bran mixture and then the chocolate, each square cut into four. Fill the tins two-thirds full and bake at Gas Mark 6/200°C/400°F for about 20 minutes, until cooked through but not hard. Make the muffins in batches.

If possible, serve the muffins straight from the oven, or warm them through just before you eat them.

Tip: Ensure the teaspoons of baking powder are level; there is quite a high proportion of raising agent in this recipe, and rounded spoons will affect the taste.

Makes about 20, depending on tin size

Topping Brownies

No chocolate cookery book would be complete without this recipe, and these Brownies are just as they should be, richly chocolate-flavoured and moist.

175 g (6 oz) margarine
25 g (1 oz) Cadbury's Bournville cocoa
175 g (6 oz) dark soft brown sugar
2 eggs
50 g (2 oz) self-raising flour
50 g (2 oz) walnuts or pecan nuts
100 g bar of Cadbury's Bournville chocolate

an 18 cm (7-inch), deep, square tin, greased lightly and base-lined

Melt 50 g (2 oz) of the fat in a pan and stir in the cocoa. Cream the remaining margarine with the sugar. Gradually beat in the eggs and cocoa mixture. Fold in the flour, chopped nuts and half the chocolate, with each square cut into four or six. Turn the mixture into the tin, smooth over the surface and then grate the remaining chocolate over the top. Bake at Gas Mark 4/180°C/350°F for about 45 minutes, until cooked but still moist. Cool in the tin. Later turn out and cut into 9 squares.

Serve the Brownies as they are or cut into larger squares and top with generous scoops of ice cream.

Makes 9   *Pictured on the back cover*

Frosting for Brownies

Brownies with a frosting topping are also popular. Omit the grated chocolate on top of the uncooked mixture but otherwise, make up the Brownie mixture as the recipe opposite.

50 g Cadbury's Bournville chocolate
65 g (2½ oz butter)
20 ml (1 tablespoon) Cadbury's Bournville cocoa
60 ml (3 tablespoons) milk or cream
225 g (8 oz) icing sugar

Break the chocolate into a pan and slowly melt it with the butter, cocoa and milk or cream. When quite smooth, leave to cool before beating in the icing sugar; beat hard so that it thickens and becomes a luscious frosting. A flavouring essence may be added at this stage for variety. Spread the frosting over the Brownies in the tin before you cut them.

Swiss Tarts

Sometimes called Viennese Whirls.

125 g (4 oz) slightly salted butter, softened
25 g (1 oz) icing sugar, plus a little extra, sieved
125 g (4 oz) plain flour
40 ml (2 tablespoons) Cadbury's drinking chocolate
about 60 ml (3 tablespoons) apricot or red jam
a packet of Cadbury's milk chocolate Buttons

paper cake cases
a baking or patty tin tray
a piping bag with a star nozzle attached

Have the butter at room temperature so that it can be creamed with the sieved icing sugar. When really light, fold in half the flour and drinking chocolate and beat again, hard, before beating in the remaining dry ingredients to a piping consistency. Fill the piping bag, and then pipe whirls in the paper cases, starting from the centre, making about eight (Fig. 1). Place them either close together on the baking tray to stop them spreading, or individually in the patty tins. Bake at Gas Mark 5/190°C/375°F for 20–25 minutes. Leave until firm enough to handle before lifting off to cool.

Dust with icing sugar, spoon a little jam into the centres, with a chocolate Button on top.

Fig. 1 *Use a circular movement when piping, from the centre out*

Tip: Use a vegetable nozzle, not an icing pipe, which would be too fine for this very 'short' mixture.

Makes about 8   *Pictured on the back cover*

Tutti-Frutti Cake

A traditional Italian lemon cake containing a filling of chopped mixed fruit; this is often served at festival times.

FOR THE CAKE
125 g (4 oz) butter or margarine
125 g (4 oz) caster sugar
2 eggs
125 g (4 oz) self-raising flour, sieved
grated rind of 1 large lemon
FOR THE FILLING AND DECORATION
225 g (8 oz) cream cheese
142 ml (¼ pint) whipping cream
50 g (2 oz) icing sugar
40 ml (2 tablespoons) orange liqueur or orange juice
25 g (1 oz) mixed glacé fruit, chopped finely
FOR THE ICING
200 g bar of Cadbury's Bournville chocolate
5 ml (1 teaspoon) strong instant coffee
125 g (4 oz) butter
5 Cadbury's Flake from the family box
4 mixed coloured glacé cherries, quartered

a ½ kg (1 lb) loaf tin, greased and strip-lined
2 piping bags fitted with small and larger pipes

To make the cake, beat the butter and sugar together until light and creamy. Add the eggs, one at a time, beating thoroughly after each addition. Fold in the sieved flour, and then the lemon rind. Turn the mixture into the tin and bake at Gas Mark 3/170°C/325°F for 50–60 minutes, until well risen and nicely browned. Turn out and cool on a wire tray. Later cut into three even layers.

Make the filling by beating the cream cheese with 20 ml (1 tablespoon) of cream, the icing sugar and the liqueur or juice, until it is quite smooth. Spread this over two layers, sprinkle with chopped glacé fruit and sandwich the cake back together again. Lift on to an oblong plate.

Melt the chocolate for the icing with the coffee, butter and 40 ml (2 tablespoons) of water, stirring slowly until smooth. Allow to cool before beating in the remaining cream so that it is thick enough to coat the cake. Chill if necessary to speed up the process.

Place a third of the icing in the piping bag, spread the remainder neatly over the cake. Pipe a small border round the base and top of the cake, using the smaller pipe. Evenly space the Flake along the top. Lightly whip the remaining cream and then pipe slightly larger whirls, using the larger pipe, between the Flake. Pop a piece of cherry on each whirl.

Tip: Substitute an Italian liqueur for the water in the icing.

Serves 6–8

Tuti-Frutti Cake

Pavlova

FOR THE MERINGUE
3 egg whites
225 g (8 oz) caster sugar
20 ml (1 tablespoon) cornflour, sieved
25 g (1 oz) Cadbury's Bournville cocoa
5 ml (1 teaspoon) vinegar
FOR THE TOPPING AND DECORATION
150 g Cadbury's Bournville chocolate
142 ml (¼ pint) double cream
150 g (5 oz) carton of natural yogurt
1 kiwi fruit, peeled and sliced
1 banana, sliced
1 red apple, cored and sliced
1 orange, peeled and segmented
chocolate leaves (page 12)

baking parchment
a baking tray

For the meringue base, mark a 23 cm (9-inch) circle on baking parchment and lay it upside-down on the baking tray. Whisk the egg whites until very stiff; gradually add the sugar and continue whisking until stiff again. Fold in the sieved cornflour, with the cocoa and vinegar. Spread the meringue over the marked circle, making it as flat as possible and trying to keep it within the drawn outline. Bake in a cool oven at Gas Mark 1/140°C/275°F for about 2 hours. Leave to cool on the tray and then carefully peel off the paper. Place the Pavlova on an attractive plate.

For the topping, melt the chocolate. Whip the cream and yogurt together until thick, fold in the cooled chocolate and then spread the cream over the meringue base. Decorate with the prepared fruit and chocolate leaves.

Note: Assemble the dessert no more than an hour before serving.

Serves 8

Iced Chocolate Drink

60 ml (3 tablespoons) Cadbury's drinking chocolate
568 ml (1 pint) milk
150 g (5 oz) natural yogurt
5 scoops of ice cream
20–40 ml (1–2 tablespoons) Tia Maria liqueur
20 ml (1 tablespoon) caster sugar (optional)
4–5 spoonsful whipped cream
4 or 5 Cadbury's Flake from the family box

Mix the drinking chocolate with just a little milk and heat to cook briefly. Put the remaining milk with the other ingredients, except the cream and Flake, into a liquidiser with the drinking chocolate; blend thoroughly. Divide the drink between tall glasses and serve each topped with whipped cream and a Flake. Drink through wide straws.

Serves 4–5   *Pictured on page 59*

Pavlova (opposite)

Velvet Chocolate Drink

The ultimate in luxury, this hot drink literally melts as you drink it and is for special occasions.

568 ml (1 pint) milk
100 g bar of Cadbury's Bournville chocolate
40 ml (2 tablespoons) Cadbury's Bournville cocoa
2.5 ml (¹/₂ teaspoon) ground nutmeg
80 ml (4 tablespoons) brandy
80 ml (4 tablespoons) whipped cream
4 Cadbury's Flake from the family box

Gently heat the milk with the broken-up chocolate so that it is melted. Whisk in the cocoa, nutmeg and brandy, boiling briefly. Either whisk so that it is frothy or liquidise the drink, then pour into four cups. Top with whipped cream and crushed Flake, or serve the whole Flake in each hot drink so that they melt gradually.

Serves 4   *Pictured on the back cover*

Cup Cakes

FOR THE CAKES
125 g (4 oz) margarine
125 g (4 oz) caster or soft brown sugar
2 eggs
125 g (4 oz) self-raising flour
25 g (1 oz) Cadbury's Bournville cocoa
FOR THE ICING
50 g (2 oz) butter
40–80 ml (2–4 tablespoons) water
225 g (8 oz) icing sugar
25 g (1 oz) Cadbury's Bournville cocoa
a packet of Cadbury's creamy-white Buttons

20 paper cake cases
a baking tray (or bun tins)

For the cakes, cream the margarine and sugar together until lighter in colour and texture. Gradually beat in the eggs. Fold in the flour and cocoa, sieved together. Place a good teaspoon of the mixture into each paper case and then place them close together on a baking tray to help prevent spreading (or put them in bun tin trays to give support). Bake at Gas Mark 5/190°F/375°F for 12–15 minutes, until springy to the touch yet cooked. Cool on a wire tray.

Make the icing by melting the butter in the water. Sieve in the icing sugar and cocoa, and beat until smooth and really glossy, adding extra water if necessary. Spoon or pour a little icing on to each cake, lightly tapping it as you do to settle the icing evenly. Stick a Button in the centre of each. Should the icing begin to form a skin before you have finished, beat it again. Leave the icing to set.

Makes about 20

No-Bake Biscuit Slice

FOR THE BISCUIT BASE
125 g (4 oz) butter.
40 ml (2 tablespoons) golden syrup
225 g (8 oz) sweet biscuits
25 g (1 oz) raisins
50 g (2 oz) no-soak apricots, chopped
200 g bar of Cadbury's Bournville chocolate
FOR THE FUDGE ICING
25 g (1 oz) butter
175 g (6 oz) icing sugar

a ¹/₂ kg (1 lb) loaf tin, strip-lined with foil

For the base, melt the butter and syrup in a saucepan. Crush the biscuits, but not too finely, and then stir them into the pan with the raisins, chopped apricots and 150 g of the chocolate, each square cut into four. Stir well together and then press the mixture into the tin and leave in the refrigerator overnight to harden.

Make the icing by melting the remaining chocolate with 40 ml (2 tablespoons) of water and the butter. Heat gently until quite smooth. Beat in the icing sugar off the heat, and continue beating hard with a wooden spoon until the icing is quite thick and silky smooth. The more you beat, the thicker it becomes as it cools. Turn out the biscuit base and swirl the fudge icing attractively over it. Lift on to a board and allow the icing to harden a little before cutting into slices.

Tip: The remains of biscuits at the end of the barrel are ideal for this recipe as there is usually a mixture – use crumbs and all. Digestive or other rough-textured biscuits are also excellent; choose shortbread for a very special treat.

Serves 6

Flaky Éclairs

Nothing is nicer than a freshly made chocolate éclair and these have the added surprise of Cadbury's Flake.

FOR THE CHOUX PASTRY
125 ml (¼ pint) water
50 g (2 oz) butter or margarine
65 g (2½ oz) plain flour, sieved
2 × size 2 eggs, beaten
FOR THE FILLING
142 ml (¼ pint) whipping cream
1 Cadbury's Flake from the family box
FOR THE ICING
100 g bar of Cadbury's Bournville chocolate
a good knob of butter
10 ml (2 teaspoons) bland salad oil

a piping bag with a plain 1.5 cm (¾-inch) nozzle
a baking tray, floured lightly

For the choux pastry, measure the water into the saucepan, and then melt the fat in it before bringing it to the boil. Immediately take the pan off the heat and shoot in the flour all at once. Stir the mixture into a thick paste. Gradually add the beaten eggs, beating hard with a wooden spoon between additions. The pastry should have a real gloss, be absolutely smooth and be coming away from the pan when it is ready. Fill the piping bag with the choux pastry, which may be left for up to 24 hours at this stage.

Pipe eight even-sized lengths on the baking tray, using a Flake as a guide and spacing them well apart. Bake on a rising heat, starting at Gas Mark 4/180°C/350°F for 10 minutes, and increasing the heat to Gas Mark 5/190°C/375°F for a further 10 minutes. Finally increase the heat again to Gas Mark 6/200°C/400°F for about 10 minutes so that the éclairs are well risen, golden brown and firm. Carefully remove from the tray and make a small slit in the side of each for the steam to escape. Leave to cool completely.

For the filling, lightly whip the cream until it holds its shape. Cut each Flake in half lengthways. Split the éclairs along one side to open them up and then either spoon or pipe the cream inside and lay a piece of Flake in the centre.

For the icing, break up the chocolate and melt it with the butter and oil over a gentle heat, stirring until blended together and smooth. Cool the icing until it is thick enough to coat the top of each éclair. Serve the éclairs the same day as they are made.

Tip: Stir two spoonsful of chocolate icing into the whipped cream for a change and add a little orange flavoured liqueur for a special dessert.

The éclairs are also nice with ice cream and Cadbury's Flake in the centre, instead of cream.

Makes 8   *Pictured on the back cover*

Rich Chocolate Mousse

200 g bar of Cadbury's Bournville chocolate
284 ml (½ pint) whipping cream
10 ml (2 teaspoons) dry instant coffee
4 egg yolks
40 ml (2 tablespoons) Tia Maria coffee liqueur
4 Cadbury's Flake from the family box

8 small serving glasses

Break the chocolate into a blender goblet. Heat the cream with the coffee to boiling point, then pour into the blender and liquidise for 1 minute, until the chocolate has melted. Add the egg yolks and liqueur, blend for a further 30 seconds and turn into a bowl. Refrigerate for at least an hour until cold and thick.

Whisk the mixture vigorously until light and fluffy, then stir in two roughly crumbled Flake. Divide the mixture between individual glasses and chill well, before serving each one decorated with half a Flake.

Tip: The final whisking is all-important to the texture. Beat for at least 5 minutes with an electric mixer until the mousse becomes thicker and slightly paler in colour.

Serves 6−8   *Pictured on the front cover*

Chocolate Fudge

50 g (2 oz) butter
40 ml (2 tablespoons) honey
25 g (1 oz) Cadbury's Bournville cocoa
450 g (1 lb) granulated sugar
200 g (7 oz) condensed milk
80 ml (4 tablespoons) water

an 18 cm (7-inch) square, shallow tin, greased lightly

Measure all the ingredients into a fairly large, thick-based pan. Stir over a very gentle heat until the sugar has completely dissolved; it should not feel at all grainy – this is most important. Now bring to the boil and cook steadily, not too fast, at a just-rolling boil, until the soft-ball stage is reached (114°C/238°F). Check with a sugar thermometer if you have one, otherwise drop a little into a saucer of cold water to see if it hardens to the right consistency, but do not be tempted to take it off too soon.

Take the pan off the heat and beat the fudge hard with a wooden spoon until it is nice and smooth, and thickened. It should also have a good gloss. Pour into the tin and leave to harden overnight. Cut into about 36 squares, depending on whether you like bigger or smaller pieces.

Variations: To the basic fudge, add any of the following: 125 g (4 oz) quartered glacé or maraschino cherries; 50 g (2 oz) roughly chopped nuts; the finely grated rind of ½ orange; 125 g (4 oz) raisins soaked in 40 ml (2 tablespoons) rum or 10 ml (2 teaspoons) rum essence. Or lightly fold in a packet of marshmallows just before pouring into the tin.

Makes about 36 pieces

Chocolate Fudge (Nut, Raisin and Mallow); Iced Chocolate Drink (page 54)

Fresh & Fruity

Chocolate and fruit go so well together, and these are some of the freshest ideas in the book. Try Brown Bread Beano or Bananarama when you have guests, both of which have the distinct advantage that you can make them in advance. Two of our firm favourites have to be Iceberg, which is very easy to make yet looks good when turned out, and the ever popular Golden Meringue Cake.

Bananarama

An ice-cold dessert with a distinctive banana centre and a tangy outer edge. Another of our real favourites, and one that always gets an enthusiastic reaction.

a packet (8) of trifle sponges
3 lemons
75 g (3 oz) granulated sugar
2 × size 2 eggs
125 g (4 oz) demerara sugar
3 ripe bananas
284 ml (½ pint) whipping cream
8 Cadbury's Flake from the family box
1 lemon slice (optional)

a 19 cm (7½-inch), round, deep, loose-based cake tin

Slice the sponges through the centre and then lay these thinner pieces, crumb-side upwards, on a tray. Finely grate the rinds of two of the lemons and squeeze out the juice. Sprinkle the lemon rind over the sponges. Make the lemon juice up to 125 ml (¼ pint) with water. Dissolve the granulated sugar in this liquid in a pan over a gentle heat and when clear, boil rapidly for 1 minute. Soak the sponges with this syrup.

Using an electric mixer, whisk the eggs until really frothy. In a pan, dissolve the demerara sugar in 6 tablespoons of water, stirring over a low heat until clear, and then boil for 3 minutes. Immediately whisk this syrup into the eggs, and continue whisking until quite thick and cool.

Grate the remaining lemon rind finely. Squeeze out the juice and mash it with the bananas into a purée. Whip the cream lightly until it just holds its shape, crumble in four Flake and then fold the cream into the egg mixture, with the bananas. Press the sponges firmly up the sides and on the base of the tin, ensuring they stick there. Fill the centre with the banana mixture and freeze overnight. Cover and label if to be kept – it will keep for up to a month.

Turn the dessert on to a plate, carefully running a knife round the sides to ensure it comes out of the tin. Decorate with small pieces of the remaining Flake, criss-crossed round the edge and put a twist of lemon in the centre if you like. A lemon geranium leaf also looks attractive. Allow to soften a little so that the dessert can be cut in neat wedges.

Serves 8

Golden Meringue Cake; Bananarama

Golden Meringue Cake

These cakes are always in demand and can be eaten as a cake, dessert or just with tea or coffee, or with an ice-cold chocolate drink.

FOR THE CAKE
4 × size 2 egg whites
2.5 ml (½ teaspoon) cream of tartar
20 ml (1 tablespoon) water
150 g (5 oz) caster sugar
25 g (1 oz) cornflour
50 g (2 oz) ground almonds
5 ml (1 teaspoon) vanilla essence
4 Cadbury's Flake from the family box
FOR THE FILLING AND DECORATION
4 egg yolks
2 oranges
25 g (1 oz) caster sugar
40 ml (2 tablespoons) Cointreau or orange juice
2 kiwi fruits
142 ml (¼ pint) double cream
4 Cadbury's Flake from the family box

two 19 cm (7½-inch) sandwich tins, base-lined with baking parchment

Whisk the egg whites with the cream of tartar and water until stiff – an electric mixer will help. Gradually whisk in the sugar and beat until the mixture is as stiff again. Sieve in the cornflour. Fold in the ground almonds, essence and chopped Flake, ensuring no dry patches remain. Divide the mixture evenly between the tins. Bake in a cool oven at Gas Mark 2/150°C/300°F on the lowest shelf, for 2 hours. Carefully loosen round the sides and then cool in the tin. Store in an air-tight container until required.

Make the custard filling by placing the egg yolks and finely grated rind and juice of 1 orange in a saucepan (use a double boiler if you have one). Stir continuously but gently over a low heat until it thickens. Remove from the heat before adding the Cointreau or orange juice; cool in the fridge.

Segment the remaining orange, and peel and slice the kiwi fruits; reserve eight or nine pieces of each for the top. Whip the cream and fold half into the cold custard.

Lift one meringue layer on to an attractive plate, spread over the custard and fruit and then gently press the other layer on top. Spread the remaining cream over the top. Decorate with the fruit and the Flake, cut in half lengthways and arranged like the spokes of a wheel.

If there is any left, the meringue goes 'soggy' and is superb the second day, but keep in the fridge because of the cream.

Tip: Peel the kiwi fruit and then cut it up in an egg slicer for really quickly-prepared, even slices.

Serves 8

Lemon Layer Pudding

Lemon Layer Pudding

50 g (2 oz) butter
125 g (4 oz) caster sugar, plus a little extra
finely grated rind and juice of 2 lemons
2 eggs, separated
50 g (2 oz) self-raising flour, sifted
275 ml (½ pint) milk
5 Cadbury's Flake from the family box

a 1.1-litre (2-pint) ovenproof dish, greased lightly
a roasting tin

Cream the butter and sugar together well. Add the finely grated lemon rind and strained juice. Beat the egg yolks, sifted flour and milk together (the mixture may look curdled at this stage). Whisk the egg whites quite stiffly and then fold them into the mixture, with three crumbled-up Flake. Pour the mixture into the prepared dish and stand it in the roasting tin half-filled with warm water. Bake at Gas Mark 4/180°C/350°F for about 45 minutes, until golden brown and springy to touch.

Sprinkle with caster sugar and crumble over the remaining Flake. Serve immediately, with single cream or thin custard if liked.

Serves 4–5

Banana Creole

Hot bananas have a flavour all their own. We also give a variation on Poires Belle Helene that you must try.

4 small bananas
lemon juice
1 orange
60 ml (3 tablespoons) Cadbury's Bournville cocoa
60 ml (3 tablespoons) muscovado brown sugar
grated nutmeg
40 ml (2 tablespoons) dark rum
80 ml (4 tablespoons) whipped cream

an ovenproof dish, buttered

Peel the bananas, sprinkle them with a little lemon juice and lay them in the dish. Grate half the orange rind into a small pan, squeeze out the juice and heat slowly with the cocoa, sugar and grated nutmeg; stir without boiling. Add the rum and then pour over the bananas and bake at Gas Mark 6/200°C/400°F for 15 minutes until cooked. Serve with whipped cream.

Tip: Fresh pears are also excellent but they take a little longer to cook. Peel, core and quarter the pears. If they are not really ripe, cook the pears at a lower temperature, Gas Mark 3/170°C/325°F, for up to an hour until they are cooked but not mushy. Serve hot or cold, preferably with a good dollop of ice cream.

Serves 2

Flake Fruit Tang

a packet (8) of trifle sponges
225 g (8 oz) blackberries, raspberries or other soft
  fruit
150 g (5 oz) caster sugar
568 ml (1 pint) natural yogurt
6 Cadbury's Flake from the family box
142 ml (¼ pint) whipping cream, whipped lightly

a 1.1-litre (2-pint) ovenproof dish

Slice the sponges in half and cover the base of the dish. Place the fruit on top. Mix the sugar into the yogurt, then add half the Flake, crumbled up. Pour this over the fruit, bake at Gas Mark 4/180°C/350°F for about 55 minutes, until the topping has set. Allow to cool completely before spreading the lightly whipped cream over the top. Crumble the remaining Flake randomly on top.

Tip: Use canned fruit if fresh fruit is not available, although the flavour will naturally not be as sharp. Try to mix some fresh fruit in with the canned even if it is only a chopped apple.

Serves 4

Iceberg

The easiest imaginable recipe to make, this is especially good when fresh lemons are really juicy and at their best. The mixture is also suitable to fill a flan biscuit crust, but you need a deep flan dish not a very shallow one.

397 g (14 oz) can of condensed milk
3 × size 2 eggs, separated
3 juicy lemons
142 ml (¼ pint) double cream
7 Cadbury's Flake from the family box

a 1 kg (2 lb) loaf tin, strip-lined

Chill the condensed milk overnight in the fridge. Whisk the egg yolks and condensed milk together until thick, using an electric or rotary whisk. Finely grate the rind of two lemons, ensuring no white pith is included as this will make it bitter. Squeeze out the juice and stir it into the mixture, with the rind. Whisk the egg whites stiffly, then whip the cream until it just holds its shape. Fold both in, with three chopped Flake. Turn the mixture into the lined tin and freeze overnight.

Dip the tin quickly into hot water to loosen the dessert and use the paper to ease it out, turning it on to a plate. Cut three Flake in half lengthways and lay them along the top; put segments of the remaining lemon in between. Serve in slices.

Serves 6 generously

Brown Bread Beano

Layers of crisp breadcrumbs, fruit and cream combine to make a dessert for friends and family alike. We prefer it left for a day or so to get 'soggy' but others like it 'fresh and fruity'.

125 g (4 oz) fresh brown breadcrumbs
150 g (5 oz) demerara sugar
50 g (2 oz) Cadbury's drinking chocolate
5 ml (1 teaspoon) dry instant coffee
142 ml (¼ pint) double cream
142 ml (¼ pint) single cream or natural yogurt
a tin, jar or sachet of fruit pie filling
5 ml (1 teaspoon) lemon juice
50 g bar of Cadbury's Bournville chocolate, grated

Mix the breadcrumbs, sugar, drinking chocolate and coffee together. Whip the creams or cream and yogurt together, not too stiffly. Spread a little cream in the base of a pretty glass bowl and then make layers in this order: breadcrumb mixture; cream; fruit (sharpened with the lemon juice) in the centre; breadcrumbs; cream on top. Cover with grated chocolate and then chill overnight, or for 24 hours which is even better.

Serves 6–8

Raspberry Shortcake

100 g bar of Cadbury's Bournville chocolate
125 g (4 oz) plain flour
125 g (4 oz) cornflour
175 g (6 oz) butter
75 g (3 oz) caster sugar
125 g (4 oz) ground almonds
finely grated rind of 1 orange
TO COMPLETE
284 ml (½ pint) whipping cream
60 ml (3 tablespoons) raspberry fromage frais
175 g (6 oz) fresh raspberries
8 Cadbury's Flake from the family box

a pastry wheel (optional)
two baking trays, dusted with flour
a 5 cm (2-inch) fluted cutter
a piping bag and star pipe

Melt the chocolate. Sieve the flour and cornflour together, rub in the butter, and then add the sugar, ground almonds, grated orange rind and cooled chocolate. Knead the dough lightly until smooth and divide it equally into three. Roll each piece into a rectangle measuring 7.5 × 25 cm (3 × 10 inches), trimming the edges with a pastry wheel if you have one. Lift on to the baking trays. Re-roll the scraps of dough, cut out four fluted biscuits using the cutter and then halve them and place on the baking tray. Chill the shortcake for an hour before baking it at Gas Mark 3/ 170°C/325°F for ½ hour. Cool on the baking trays.

To complete, whip the cream and fromage frais together, fill the piping bag, then pipe a line down the centre of one shortcake layer. Pipe the remaining cream over the other two layers. Reserve seven raspberries, place the remainder over the two shortcake layers, then layer up all three on an attractive plate. Place the Flake on top and arrange the half-circle biscuits and raspberries in between. Assemble a couple of hours before required as it is then easier to slice.

Tip: When rolling out, keep the dough in an oblong shape and measure frequently, so the shortbread strips are as even and thick as possible. One layer may be brushed with milk and sprinkled with chopped almonds before baking, which gives a crunchy texture.

Serves 6–8

Grape Delight

100 g bar of Cadbury's Bournville chocolate
25 g (1 oz) muscovado sugar
142 ml (¼ pint) whipping cream
150 g (5 oz) natural yogurt
350 g (12 oz) green grapes

Grate the chocolate and then mix it with the sugar. Whip the cream and yogurt until stiff. Halve the grapes and pip if necessary; reserve a few for decoration and layer the remainder with the chocolate and cream in an attractive dish or individual glasses, ending with chocolate. Refrigerate overnight. Decorate with grapes.

Serves 6–8

Brown Bread Beano; Raspberry Shortcake

St Clement's Peak

Like a Baked Alaska but with a really fresh-tasting, orange, sorbet-type mound under the lightly cooked meringue.

FOR THE FILLING
1 large orange, preferably thin-skinned
175 ml (6 fl oz) orange juice
125 g (4 oz) caster sugar
100 ml (4 fl oz) water
125 g (4 oz) golden syrup
200 ml (7 fl oz) milk
FOR THE BASE
100 g bar of Cadbury's Bournville chocolate
75 g (3 oz) butter
5 ml (1 teaspoon) dry instant coffee
3 eggs, separated
75 g (3 oz) ground almonds
75 g (3 oz) caster sugar
2 oranges
FOR THE MERINGUE TOPPING
2 egg whites
125 g (4 oz) caster sugar

a 20 cm (8-inch), round, loose-based cake tin
an ovenproof plate on a baking tray

For the filling, wipe the orange, chop roughly, remove the pips and place in a liquidiser. Add the juice and process to a pulp. Dissolve the sugar in the water over a gentle heat and when clear, stir in the golden syrup and bring to the boil for a minute. Add to the orange and strain into a bowl, pressing through as much as possible. Stir in the milk. Pour into a metal container, if possible, to speed up the freezing, and freeze for at least 3 hours or until hard.

For the base, finely grate two squares of chocolate and reserve for decoration. Melt the remaining chocolate with the butter and coffee. Stir in the egg yolks and ground almonds. Whisk the egg whites stiffly, fold in the sugar and whisk until as stiff again and glossy. Fold this into the chocolate mixture, pour into the tin and bake at Gas Mark 3/170°C/325°F for about 55 minutes. Turn off the oven and leave the base to cool. Peel and segment the oranges, then freeze them on a baking tray.

Place the chocolate base on an ovenproof plate on a baking tray. Scoop out the orange mixture and pile it

St Clement's Peak

on top of the chocolate base. Arrange the frozen orange segments round the edge. Whisk the egg whites for the meringue topping stiffly, fold in the sugar and whisk again until glossy. Cover the frozen orange mixture with the meringue; do not cover the orange segments, leave them showing. Place in a very hot oven, Gas Mark 8/230°C/450°F, for 3–5 minutes until nicely golden brown. Sprinkle with the grated chocolate and serve immediately.

Tip: As the whole orange is liquidised, this recipe can have a strong pith flavour, depending on the orange. To avoid this, finely grate the orange rind, peel off the white pith and liquidise the orange flesh.

Serves 6–7

Tangy Choco-Lime Mousse

A slightly different way to present a mousse. Take care with lining the tin and the rest is easy.

---

200 g (7 oz) cream cheese
25 g (1 oz) caster sugar
142 ml (¼ pint) whipping cream, whipped
2 limes
FOR THE MOUSSE FILLING
200 g bar of Cadbury's Bournville chocolate
15 ml (3 teaspoons) gelatine
25 g (1 oz) caster sugar
4 eggs, separated
8 sponge fingers
40 ml (2 tablespoons) rum
1 lime, to decorate

---

a 1 kg (2 lb) loaf tin, strip lined with foil

Cream the cream cheese, sugar and whipped cream together until smooth and thick. Finely grate the rind of the limes and fold it into the cheese mixture. Spread this quickly over the base and up the sides of the tin as evenly as possible. Chill. Squeeze the juice out of the two limes and make it up to 100 ml (5 tablespoons) with water. Pour into a heatproof bowl.

Melt 50 g of the chocolate for the mousse and use it to make chocolate leaves (page 12). Break up the remaining chocolate and melt it with the lime juice over a pan of hot water or in a microwave on DEFROST for 4 minutes. Dissolve the gelatine in 40 ml (2 tablespoons) of hot water until quite clear (or in a microwave on HIGH for 30 seconds), then stir it into the chocolate mixture, with the sugar and egg yolks. Whisk the egg whites stiffly and carefully fold them in; pour the mixture into the tin.

Dip each sponge finger into the rum and place, sugar-side down, on top of the mousse. Leave to set.

Carefully remove from the tin and place on an oblong dish. Decorate the top with the chocolate leaves and thin pieces of lime.

Serves 8   *Pictured on page 1*

Definitely Different

This chapter is full of recipes that are out of the ordinary, either in the way they are made, in the presentation or even in their unusual ingredients.

These are for special occasions perhaps, but we are quite sure that one or more will soon earn a place in your collection of favourite recipes.

Peanut Passion Cake

A traditional cake recipe that is also very much up to date. The cake has quite a close texture.

FOR THE CAKE
3 eggs
175 g (6 oz) soft brown sugar
175 g (6 oz) butter, melted
7.5 ml (1½ teaspoons) vanilla essence
350 g (12 oz) self-raising flour
5 ml (1 teaspoon) baking powder
225 g (8 oz) carrots, peeled and grated
25 g (1 oz) walnut pieces, chopped
FOR THE FILLING AND DECORATION
340 g (12 oz) jar of smooth peanut butter
50 g (2 oz) butter
125 g (4 oz) icing sugar, sieved
FOR THE ICING
200 g bar of Cadbury's Bournville chocolate
284 ml (½ pint) double cream
5 ml (1 teaspoon) dry instant coffee

a 20 cm (8-inch), deep, round, cake tin, greased and base-lined
a piping bag with a star pipe

For the cake, whisk the eggs and sugar until light and fluffy; slowly whisk in the butter and essence. Fold in the sieved dry ingredients, and prepared carrots and walnuts. Turn the mixture into the tin, hollow out the centre really well and bake at Gas Mark 4/180°C/350°F for about 1 hour until cooked, testing the centre with a warm skewer. Cool before turning out.

For the filling, beat the peanut butter with the butter and then beat in the icing sugar, making it quite smooth. Place a large tablespoon of this in the piping bag. Slice the cake into three layers and spread them with the peanut filling; sandwich back together.

Make the icing by gently heating the broken-up chocolate, cream and coffee in a pan. When melted, take off the heat and beat until absolutely smooth. Chill until the icing is thick enough to swirl over the cake. Pipe a decorative edge with the reserved peanut mixture.

Note: 225 g (8 oz) self-raising wholemeal flour may be substituted for part of the white flour, but using all wholemeal flour tends to make the cake rather heavy.

Serves 8–10

Peanut Passion Cake; Cherry Leaf Cake

Cherry Leaf Cake

Watch out for the unusual method of making this recipe, which would be ideal as a cake, or dessert perhaps served with freshly stewed pears.

150 g Cadbury's Bournville chocolate
175 g (6 oz) cream cheese
50 g (2 oz) butter, softened
675 g (1½ lb) icing sugar, sieved
50 ml (2 fl oz) milk
FOR THE CAKE
50 g (2 oz) butter
2 × size 2 eggs
175 g (6 oz) plain flour
25 g (1 oz) Cadbury's Bournville cocoa
2.5 ml (½ teaspoon) baking powder
2.5 ml (½ teaspoon) bicarbonate of soda
175 ml (6 fl oz) milk
TO COMPLETE
75 g (3 oz) cream cheese
142 ml (¼ pint) double cream
60 ml (3 tablespoons) jam
10 glacé cherries
caster sugar

two 19 cm (7½-inch) sandwich tins, greased and base-lined
a piping bag and star pipe

Make ten chocolate leaves with the chocolate, as described on page 12.

Beat the cream cheese and butter together and then alternately beat in the sieved icing sugar and milk. Blend in the melted chocolate remaining from the leaf decorations (about 100 g). Weigh out 350 g (12 oz) of mixture into a bowl; cover the remainder and put in the fridge.

Now make the cake by creaming the remaining chocolate mixture with the butter, eggs, sieved dry ingredients and the milk. Beat really well and then divide the mixture between the tins. Bake at Gas Mark 4/ 180°C/350°F for about 50 minutes, until cooked. Turn out and cool.

To complete the cake, soften the cream cheese for the icing and gradually whisk in the cream until stiff. Sandwich the cakes together with the jam and half the cream mixture. Lift the cake on to a plate. Place the remaining cream mixture in the piping bag. Spread the reserved chocolate mixture all over the cake, getting it to the right consistency so that it can be marked into lines. Pipe a border of cream mixture. Wash the cherries, toss in the sugar and place at even intervals round the edge with the chocolate leaves. Keep cool until required.

Serves 8

Tempting Crêpe Tier

An unusual dessert that is certain to be a talking point. Serve in neat wedges so that the attractive layers show.

FOR THE BATTER
100 g bar of Cadbury's Bournville chocolate
175 ml (7 fl oz) water
142 ml (¼ pint) single cream
40 ml (2 tablespoons) sugar
150 g (5 oz) plain flour, sieved
50 g (2 oz) soft margarine
3 × size 2 eggs
FOR THE FILLING AND DECORATION
225 g (8 oz) cottage cheese
225 g (8 oz) cream cheese
284 ml (½ pint) double cream
60 ml (3 tablespoons) Cointreau or orange juice
20 ml (1 tablespoon) caster sugar
2 oranges
chocolate leaves (see page 12)

a 20 cm (8-inch) frying-pan or crêpe pan

Make the crêpe batter by breaking up the chocolate and melting it in a pan with the water and cream. Pour the liquid into a blender or food processor, add the remaining batter ingredients and then process until absolutely smooth. Strain into a jug and allow to rest in the fridge for about 20 minutes.

Heat a crêpe pan, or frying-pan, with a little oil. Pour in about 2 tablespoons of batter, just enough to cover the base of the pan thinly; pour any excess batter back into the jug. Cook the crêpe until nicely browned and then flip it over and cook the other side. Turn out on to a clean tea towel. Repeat the process, making 12–15 in the same way. You can make these a day in advance and keep cool until required, or you can freeze them. Put greaseproof paper or special layering paper in between each one, so that they do not stick together.

Sieve the cottage cheese into a bowl, beat in the cream cheese, or work in a food processor until smooth. Lightly whip the cream and stir it in. Gradually mix in the liqueur or orange juice and the sugar. Finely grate the rind of one orange then peel and segment the flesh. Add both the rind and fruit to the cheese mixture. Segment the remaining orange for the decoration. Spread cheese mixture on all the pancakes and then layer them on a plate. Complete with the orange segments and chocolate leaves. Chill before serving in slices so that the layers show, with a thin chocolate sauce if liked.

Serves 8

Scrumptious Slice

370 g (13 oz) puff pastry
225 g (8 oz) marzipan
75 g (3 oz) glacé cherries
75 g (3 oz) desiccated coconut
2 egg whites
8 Cadbury's Flake from the family box
caster sugar

a baking tray, greased lightly

Roll the pastry into a rectangle measuring about 25 × 30 cm (10 × 12 inches). Roll the marzipan into a slightly smaller rectangle, to fit on top. Chop the cherries, mix with the coconut and enough lightly beaten egg white to bind the mixture together. Spread this over the marzipan. Lay the Flake in pairs down the centre.

Dampen the pastry edges, fold the two long sides together and seal well, then close both ends. Lift on to the baking tray with the join underneath, brush with

Tempting Crepe Tier; Hogmanay Harmony (page 78); Scrumptious Slice

egg white and sprinkle with sugar. Mark diagonal lines on the top but do not cut through. Bake at Gas Mark 8/230°C/450°F for about 15 minutes until golden brown and nicely rounded. (Watch carefully the first time you make it as each oven is different.) If burning at all, turn round in the oven or lay a butter paper on top. Serve in slices, warm or cold. It is at its best more or less straight out of the oven.

Tip: Allow a few minutes extra cooking time from frozen. When the colour is right, it should be cooked through.

Serves 6–8

Meringue Gâteau

A very special recipe, though it takes a little time.

FOR THE MERINGUE
2 egg whites
175 g (6 oz) caster sugar
50 g (2 oz) chopped almonds
20 ml (1 tablespoon) cornflour, sieved
50 g (2 oz) desiccated coconut
FOR THE MOUSSE
3 egg yolks
50 g (2 oz) caster sugar
200 g bar of Cadbury's Bournville chocolate
125 ml (¼ pint) milk
40 ml (2 tablespoons) brandy
10 ml (2 teaspoons) gelatine
284 ml (½ pint) double cream
1 egg white, whisked stiffly
TO DECORATE
75 g (3 oz) whole almonds

a 19 cm (7-inch) square, deep, loose-based cake tin, greased and base-lined

Whisk the egg whites until stiff, and then whisk in the sugar and continue whisking until as stiff again. Stir the almonds into the meringue mixture, and then the cornflour and coconut. Turn into the prepared tin, levelling the surface. Bake at Gas Mark 4/180°C/350°F for 1 hour. When cooked, carefully loosen the meringue and leave to cool completely in the tin.

Beat the egg yolks and sugar for the mousse together until pale. Melt half the chocolate in the milk, bring to the boil and stir in the egg mixture and brandy. Dissolve the gelatine in a little hot water until quite clear and then slowly stir it into the chocolate mixture. Leave to thicken, stirring occasionally.

Whip *half* the cream until it holds its shape. Fold it into the chocolate mixture, with the stiffly whisked egg white. Pour over the meringue base in the tin and refrigerate overnight to set.

Carefully heat the remaining chocolate and cream together, stirring until the chocolate is melted and blended. Leave in a cold place until the icing is thick enough to coat the back of a spoon. Pour half on top of the mousse in the tin and refrigerate for a couple of hours until set.

Reserve eight whole almonds, roughly chop the remainder and brown them under the grill. Carefully lift the gâteau out of the tin on to a plate or board, remembering to peel off the paper. Spread the remaining icing around the sides of the cake and press on the almonds. Finally, decorate with the whole almonds.

Serves 8–10

Moonlight Magic

Evoking memories of an Italian holiday, this could be described as chocolate-flavoured frozen Zabaglione on a rich base.

FOR THE BASE
100 g bar of Cadbury's Bournville chocolate
75 g (3 oz) butter
5 ml (1 teaspoon) dry instant coffee
5 ml (1 teaspoon) Cadbury's Bournville cocoa
20–40 ml (1–2 tablespoons) Marsala or sherry
3 × size 2 eggs, separated
75 g (3 oz) ground almonds
75 g (3 oz) caster sugar
FOR THE SYRUP
20 ml (1 tablespoon) caster sugar
40 ml (2 tablespoons) Marsala or sherry
FOR THE TOPPING AND DECORATION
4 egg yolks
80 ml (4 tablespoons) Marsala or sherry
284 ml (½ pint) whipping cream
40 ml (2 tablespoons) icing sugar, sieved
40 ml (2 tablespoons) Cadbury's Bournville cocoa
a fresh flower (optional)

a 20 cm (8-inch), round, loose-based cake tin,
  greased lightly

To make the base, break up the chocolate and melt it with the butter, coffee, cocoa and wine. Beat in the egg yolks and ground almonds. Whisk the egg whites until they form firm peaks and then fold in the chocolate mixture, with the sugar. Ensure there are no white patches left, but be gentle. Turn into the tin and bake at Gas Mark 3/170°C/325°F for about 50 minutes. Cool in the tin for about 10 minutes before removing. Clean the tin and then return the base to it.

Bring the syrup ingredients to the boil with a tablespoon of water and pour them evenly over the base.

For the topping, whisk the egg yolks, wine, cream and sieved icing sugar until thick, preferably using an electric mixer (it is important to obtain a good volume here). Pour over the base in the tin and freeze overnight. It may be kept for up to a month at this stage.

Slide a knife around the inner edge of the tin and then press out the dessert and place on a plate. Sieve the cocoa over the top and mark a pattern of lines with a skewer. Decorate with a pretty flower, if wished. Serve within half an hour.

Note: Use the same fortified wine throughout the recipe, i.e. Marsala *or* sherry, not a mixture.

Serves 8

Moonlight Magic; Meringue Gâteau

Hogmanay Harmony

1 orange
1 small lemon
50 g (2 oz) fine oatmeal
60 ml (3 tablespoons) whisky or sherry
40 ml (2 tablespoons) clear honey
2 egg whites
284 ml (½ pint) whipping cream
8 Cadbury's Flake from the family box

6–8 small, stylish glasses

Finely grate half the orange rind and reserve. Squeeze the juice from both fruit and strain into a saucepan, with the oatmeal, whisky or sherry and honey. Stir over a gentle heat as it thickens, then cool completely.

Whisk the egg whites quite stiffly and lightly whip the cream until it holds its shape. Fold both into the oatmeal mixture, with the orange rind. Crumble in four Flake. Divide the mixture between the glasses and stand half a Flake upright in each. Serve chilled.

Tip: Warm the fruit and roll under your palm on a hard surface to get out more juice.

Serves 6–8   Pictured on page 74

Beehive Cake

FOR THE CAKE
175 g (6 oz) soft margarine
75 g (3 oz) soft brown sugar
80 ml (4 tablespoons) clear honey
3 × size 2 eggs, separated
175 g (6 oz) self-raising flour
about 60 ml (3 tablespoons) milk
25 g (1 oz) Cadbury's Bournville cocoa
1 lemon
yellow food colouring (optional)
TO DECORATE
350 g (12 oz) Vanilla Butter Icing (page 20)
125 g (4 oz) lemon curd
1 Cadbury's Flake family box

a 1.1-litre (2-pint) ovenproof basin, greased lightly
bee and flower cake decorations (optional)

For the cake, cream the fat and sugar with 60 ml (3 tablespoons) of the honey. When well beaten, add the egg yolks, then the flour and milk to make a dropping consistency. Halve the mixture, adding cocoa to one amount, and the finely grated lemon rind and colouring, if used, to the other. Whisk the egg whites and fold half into each mixture. Spread alternate coloured layers in the basin, then hollow out the centre a little. Bake at Gas Mark 4/180°C/350°F for about 1¼ hours, until cooked through. Test with a warm skewer. Heat the remaining honey in the juice of half the lemon and then soak the cake with this, in the basin, poking it in with a skewer. Leave for 5 minutes before turning out to cool.

Cut the cake horizontally through twice, making three pieces. Have the butter icing ready. Mix a good spoonful of lemon curd into the icing. Use the remaining lemon curd to sandwich the cake together

Beehive Cake

again and place on a board or plate. Spread icing all over the cake, peaking at the top. With a really sharp knife, cut the Flake in half lengthways, and then each piece into two or three again, making different-sized pieces. Press the Flake pieces into the icing, with the larger pieces at the base graduating upwards to the smaller pieces, representing the slats of a beehive. Decorate with flowers (fresh or artificial) and a bee cake decoration or two if wished.

Note: The cake may be frozen complete on the board. Wrap loosely in foil and allow a day for thawing. This cake is a very useful shape, which can be the basis of many novelty cake ideas. Vary the honey to see which you like best – it gives the cake a lovely flavour.

Serves 8–12

Simply Satisfying

There are occasions when larger quantities are required, for a celebration or simply when a crowd of people are gathered together. Here are a selection of cakes and desserts which all look spectacular. Make them with complete confidence, they have been tested and tasted many times over!

Black Forest Extravaganza

FOR THE BASE
150 g Cadbury's Bournville chocolate
150 g (5 oz) butter
10 ml (2 teaspoons) dry instant coffee
80–100 ml (4–5 tablespoons) rum or kirsch
5 × size 2 eggs, separated
125 g (4 oz) ground almonds
125 g (4 oz) caster sugar
FOR THE TOPPING
40 ml (2 tablespoons) Kirsch (optional)
100 ml (5 tablespoons) black cherry jam
284 ml (½ pint) double cream
150 g (5 oz) carton of natural or Greek strained
   yogurt
50 g (2 oz) toasted flaked almonds
two 425 g cans of black cherries
chocolate decorations

a 25 cm (10-inch), round cake tin, 5 cm (2 inches)
   deep, greased and base-lined
a piping bag and star pipe

For the base, in a pan or microwave, gently melt the broken-up chocolate with the butter, coffee and alcohol. Beat in the egg yolks and ground almonds. Whisk the egg whites *really* stiffly and then lightly fold in the sugar. Fold in the chocolate mixture with a metal spoon, knocking out as little air as possible. Turn the mixture into the tin and bake at Gas Mark 3/ 170°C/325°F for about 1¼ hours, so that it is not soggy or runny in the middle. Turn off the oven and leave it inside to cool completely, before carefully turning out of the tin. It may now be kept or frozen.

Soak the chocolate base with the Kirsch, if using, and then spread jam over the top. Whip the cream and yogurt together and coat the top and sides with half; put the remainder in the piping bag. Press flaked almonds on the sides and pipe an edging of whipped cream. Drain off the juice and pit the cherries if necessary, then put them all over the top, on the cream. Carefully lift on to an attractive large plate. Put the chocolate decorations in place. Keep cool until required.

Tip: Pineapple rings with glacé cherries are a good alternative to the cherries. Either can be glazed with a glaze made from fruit juice.

Serves 8

Mayfair Chocolate Gâteau; Black Forest Extravaganza

Mayfair Chocolate Gâteau

A classic chocolate cake that is beautifully moist. Serve as a cake, or as a dessert with cream.

FOR THE CAKE
200 g bar of Cadbury's Bournville chocolate
250 g (9 oz) butter
250 g (9 oz) caster sugar
7.5 ml (1½ teaspoons) vanilla essence
6 × size 2 eggs, separated
225 g (8 oz) self-raising flour
50 g (2 oz) Cadbury's Bournville cocoa
FOR THE ICING AND DECORATION
50 g (2 oz) butter
75 g (3 oz) caster sugar
7.5 ml (1½ teaspoons) vanilla essence
125 g (4 oz) icing sugar
40 g (1½ oz) Cadbury's Bournville cocoa
284 ml (½ pint) double cream
150 g (5 oz) natural yogurt

a 23 cm (9-inch), round, deep cake tin, greased and base-lined
a piping bag with a star pipe
a greaseproof paper piping bag

Melt half the chocolate for the cake with 80 ml (4 tablespoons) of water. Stir until smooth, then cool. Cream the butter, sugar and essence really well together and then beat in the egg yolks and melted chocolate. Fold in the sieved flour and cocoa. Whisk the egg whites stiffly and then carefully fold them in, turn the mixture into the prepared tin, hollowing out the centre slightly. Bake at Gas Mark 4/180°C/350°F for about 1¼ hours. Test with a warm skewer to see that the centre is cooked. Turn out and cool.

For the icing, gently heat the butter, caster sugar, essence and 40 ml (2 tablespoons) water in a pan and when melted, add the sieved icing sugar and cocoa. Beat well and then leave until cold.

Lightly whip the cream and yogurt together until the mixture holds its shape, and then place four good tablespoons into the piping bag with the star pipe. Fold the remainder into the chocolate icing and chill until thickened.

Slice the cake through the middle and sandwich it back together with about 4 tablespoons of the icing. Cover the cake completely with the remaining icing, smoothing the top with a palette knife.

Grate the remaining chocolate and use some to coat the sides of the cake. Melt the remaining grated chocolate and then put it into the greaseproof paper piping bag. Snip off the end and pipe shapes on to waxed or parchment paper and leave in a cool place to set (described on page 12). Make extra shapes to allow for breakages.

Pipe whirls of cream on the top of the cake and decorate with the chocolate shapes.

Tip: If a cake has peaked in the centre, slice off the top and turn the cake upside-down before you decorate it, which gives a flatter surface to work on.

Serves about 14

Wendy's Winner

Layers of light sponge, biscuit dough and chocolate cream, covered with chocolate curls, make this 'Wendy's Winner', named after the lady who created it.

3 eggs
75 g (3 oz) caster sugar
75 g (3 oz) plain flour
25 g (1 oz) Cadbury's Bournville cocoa
FOR THE BISCUIT MIXTURE
225 g (8 oz) plain flour
40 ml (2 tablespoons) Cadbury's Bournville cocoa
50 g (2 oz) icing sugar
175 g (6 oz) butter
1 egg yolk
60 ml (3 tablespoons) brandy
60 ml (3 tablespoons) fruit juice
FOR THE ICING AND DECORATION
200 g bar of Cadbury's Bournville chocolate
75 ml (3 fl oz) milk
426 ml (¾ pint) whipping cream
150 g (5 oz) carton of natural yogurt

a 20 cm (8-inch), deep, round cake tin, greased and base-lined
2 or 3 baking trays, depending on size

Whisk the eggs and sugar for the cake together until the mixture is thick and leaves a definite trail, which will take at least 10 minutes with an electric mixer. Very gently, fold in the sieved flour and cocoa with 20 ml (1 tablespoon) warm water, making sure no dry patches remain. Turn into the tin and bake at Gas Mark 6/200°C/400°F for 30 minutes, until springy to touch. Carefully turn on to a wire tray to cool.

For the biscuit mixture, sieve the flour, cocoa and icing sugar into a bowl and then rub in the butter until it resembles breadcrumbs. Beat the egg yolk with 20 ml (1 tablespoon) of water and then add it to the mixture, binding it together to form a soft dough; knead until smooth. Divide into three, and then roll each piece on a lightly floured surface into a circle measuring 20 cm (8 inches) (use the base of the tin for accuracy). Lift on to baking trays, or make in batches. Bake at the same temperature for 10 minutes, and then cool.

Slice the cake through the centre and put one piece back into the clean tin. Stir the brandy and fruit juice together and use half to soak the cake in the tin.

Make 75 g (3 oz) of chocolate curls (as described on page 12) and reserve for the decoration. Melt the remaining chocolate with the milk and beat until smooth before leaving to cool and thicken a little. Whip the cream and yogurt together (or use all cream); fold in the chocolate. Reserve 120 ml (6 tablespoons) for the decoration, and divide the remaining cream evenly into four. Spread cream over the cake layer in the tin and then sandwich the layers of biscuit with cream in between, ending with the second cake layer. Soak this with the brandy liquid. Refrigerate at least overnight.

Carefully take the cake out of the tin and cover with the remaining chocolate cream. Lift on to a plate or board. Cover the sides of the cake with chocolate curls using a cocktail stick or skewer to lift them on so that they do not break. Sprinkle the remainder on top.

Serves 8–10

Chocolate Leaf Gâteau

It takes a little practice to get the icing looking neat using the scraper, but once you have mastered it, the cake is easily made and looks spectacular. The chocolate leaves and frosted fruit are both easy to do and would add to the appearance of any recipe.

FOR THE CAKE
50 g (2 oz) Cadbury's Bournville cocoa
175 g (6 oz) self-raising flour
2.5 ml (½ teaspoon) bicarbonate of soda
125 g (4 oz) soft margarine
225 g (8 oz) dark soft brown sugar
2 × size 2 eggs
150 g (5 oz) natural yogurt
2.5 ml (½ teaspoon) vanilla or brandy essence
60 ml (3 tablespoons) cherry brandy
TO COMPLETE
625 g (1 lb 6 oz) Chocolate Butter Icing (page 20)
50 g Cadbury's Bournville chocolate
1 egg white
4 or 5 black grapes
4 glacé cherries
50 g (2 oz) caster sugar
chocolate leaves (page 12)

a 20 cm (8-inch), round, deep cake tin, preferably loose-based, greased and base-lined
a baking tray
a serrated cake scraper
a piping bag and small star pipe

Make the cake by sifting the dry ingredients into a bowl and then adding the other ingredients, except the liqueur. Beat really well for a good 4 minutes until thoroughly creamed. Spread the mixture in the cake tin, hollow out the centre slightly and smooth over the top. Bake on a baking sheet at Gas Mark 5/190°C/375°F for 50–60 minutes, until the cake is nicely risen and cooked through. Test with a warm skewer. Allow the cake to shrink slightly before turning on to a wire tray. Moisten the cake with the cherry brandy and then cool completely.

Have the butter icing ready. Carefully cut the cake in half through the centre and sandwich back together with a little icing. Keep out about 80 ml (4 tablespoons), and spread the remaining butter icing evenly over the top and sides of the cake. Scrape the sides with the serrated cake scraper, or use a fork, or just mark into even lines. Do the same for the top. Lift the cake on to a board or plate.

Melt the chocolate and cool it slightly before stirring it into the reserved butter icing. Fill the piping bag and then pipe a neat edge round the top and bottom of the cake. If there is any left, pipe a star in the middle.

Lightly beat the egg white and brush the grapes and cherries with it before tossing them in the sugar, making sure it is only a light coating as this looks best. Leave to dry for about 10 minutes. Arrange an attractive decoration in the centre of the cake with the frosted fruit and chocolate leaves. Keep cool until required.

Tip: It is easier to use a cake turntable to do the serrating round the cake, if you have one. The cake freezes well, without the centre decoration.

Serves 8–10

Chocolate Leaf Gâteau

Chocolate Surprise

An outer casing surrounds a chocolate mousse centre, which, when cut, looks spectacular and has a taste to match. Take care to coat the tin evenly and smoothly.

350 g (12 oz) cream cheese
25 g (1 oz) caster sugar
150 g (5 oz) carton of orange yogurt
1 orange
FOR THE FILLING
200 g bar of Cadbury's Bournville chocolate
15 ml (3 teaspoons) gelatine
25 g (1 oz) caster sugar
80 ml (4 tablespoons) Cointreau or orange juice
4 eggs, separated
284 ml (½ pint) double cream
4 trifle sponges
60 ml (3 tablespoons) orange juice

an 18 cm (7-inch) square, or 20 cm (8-inch), round, loose-based cake tin, not less than 7.5 cm (3 inches) deep, lightly greased and fully lined with baking parchment

Beat together the cream cheese, sugar and 40 ml (2 tablespoons) of yogurt until smooth. Add the finely grated orange rind. Spread this mixture evenly over the base and up the sides of the tin. Chill whilst preparing the filling. Squeeze the juice from the orange and make up to 100 ml (4 fl oz) with water; pour into a heatproof bowl.

Make 25 g (1 oz) of chocolate curls (page 12) from the bar of chocolate to decorate the dessert, and then break the remaining chocolate into the bowl and melt with the orange juice over a pan of hot water or in a microwave on DEFROST for 4 minutes. Dissolve the gelatine in 40 ml (2 tablespoons) of hot water and when quite clear, stir into the chocolate, with the sugar, *half* the Cointreau or orange juice and the egg yolks. Leave until beginning to set.

Whisk the egg whites stiffly and fold into the chocolate mixture with the cream and remaining yogurt, whipped together. Pour the mixture into the prepared tin. Halve the trifle sponges and lightly press on to the mousse. Mix the orange juice and remaining Cointreau together and carefully soak the sponge. Chill for at least 6 hours or overnight.

Ease the dessert from the tin, carefully peel off the paper and then turn the dessert on to an attractive plate, with the sponge underneath. Decorate with the chocolate curls.

Tip: Brush suitable flowers, such as primroses or violets, or rose petals, with egg white and caster sugar and dry them to use as an unusual and attractive decoration.

Note: It is important to use baking parchment as greaseproof paper tends to stick. Also use a firm cream cheese so that it sets; the light varieties will not do for this recipe.

Serves 8–12   *Pictured on page 89*

Craggy Chocolate Torte

A good recipe for a large number of people; serve in slices and have a sharp fruit salad with this.

FOR THE BASE
125 g (4 oz) plain flour
75 g (3 oz) cornflour
75 g (3 oz) caster sugar
50 g (2 oz) ground almonds
175 g (6 oz) butter
FOR THE CENTRE
200 g bar of Cadbury's Bournville chocolate
5 ml (1 teaspoon) instant coffee
298 g (10½ oz) can of mandarin orange segments in natural juice
5 eggs
175 g (6 oz) caster sugar
75 g (3 oz) plain flour
10 ml (2 teaspoons) baking powder
TO COMPLETE
284 ml (½ pint) whipping cream
icing sugar

a 28 cm (11-inch), springform tin, greased lightly

Sift the flours for the base into a large bowl, add the sugar and ground almonds, then rub in the butter until the mixture resembles breadcrumbs. Knead together to form a dough, then press into the base of the tin. Bake at Gas Mark 4/180°C/350°F for 20 minutes. Leave the base in the tin.

Break up the chocolate for the centre and melt it with the coffee in 125 ml (¼ pint) of juice from the mandarins. Whisk the eggs and the sugar together in a bowl over a pan of hot water, or use an electric mixer, whisking thoroughly until quite stiff. Fold in the liquid chocolate and the sifted dry ingredients, ensuring that no dry patches remain. Pour the mixture over the base and then return to the oven and continue cooking for about a further 1¼ hours. Cool slightly before taking out of the tin; then cool completely. Freeze at this stage if required.

Lightly whip the cream. Peel off the brittle crust on top of the sponge, then break it into smaller pieces. Place the torte on a serving plate. Spread the cream over the top, swirling it attractively, then place the mandarins on top with the jagged pieces of crust standing upright in between. Dredge with sifted icing sugar.

Serves 12–16

Pictured on page 91

Choice Chocolate Cheesecake

We give two sizes for this rich and filling baked cheesecake, because it does go a long way. Serve with a generous amount of whipped cream for sheer indulgence.

FOR THE BASE
100 g bar of Cadbury's Bournville chocolate
75 g (3 oz) butter
40 ml (2 tablespoons) rum
3 eggs, separated
75 g (3 oz) ground almonds
75 g (3 oz) caster sugar
FOR THE CHEESECAKE
3 eggs, separated
125 g (4 oz) caster sugar
450 g (1 lb) cream cheese
125 ml (¼ pint) milk
40 g (1½ oz) Cadbury's Bournville cocoa
50 g (2 oz) butter
20 ml (1 tablespoon) rum
FOR THE TOPPING
142 ml (¼ pint) whipping cream

a 28 cm (11-inch), round, loose-based cake tin, greased
a baking tray

Melt the chocolate for the base in a small pan over a gentle heat, with the butter and rum. When smooth, take off the heat and stir in the egg yolks and ground almonds. Whisk the egg whites stiffly and then fold in the sugar and whisk until as stiff again. Carefully fold the mixtures together and turn into the prepared tin. Bake on a baking sheet at Gas Mark 3/170°C/325°F for 40 minutes.

Make the cheesecake by beating the yolks and sugar together really well; beat in the cream cheese and milk. Reserve a good teaspoon of cocoa, melt the butter and briefly cook the remaining cocoa in it, then add to the cheese mixture, with the rum, mixing them in thoroughly. Stiffly whisk the egg whites, fold them in, and pour over the base in the tin. Return to the oven and cook for a further 1–1¼ hours at the same temperature until set. Leave in the tin for at least 2 hours, before lifting out on to a large flat plate or cake board. Spread the top with lightly whipped cream and sieve over the reserved cocoa (or for a special occasion, substitute chocolate curls).

Tip: It is sometimes useful to have a smaller size so for a 22 cm (8½-inch) loose-based tin (to serve 8–10), halve the amount for the base but cook for the same time. Use the same quantity of cheesecake mixture, allowing 30 minutes extra cooking time because the cheesecake will be deeper.

Serves 12–16

Chocolate Surprise (page 86); Choice Chocolate Cheesecake

Iced Meringue Marseillaise

A superb gâteau to make for a special occasion: an iced mocha filling sandwiched between two layers of meringue.

FOR THE MERINGUE
4 egg whites
2.5 ml (½ teaspoon) cream of tartar
125 g (4 oz) caster sugar
5 ml (1 teaspoon) vanilla or rum essence
25 g (1 oz) cornflour, sieved
2 Cadbury's Flake
FOR THE FILLING AND DECORATION
200 g bar of Cadbury's Bournville chocolate
20 ml (1 tablespoon) dry instant coffee
60 ml (3 tablespoons) rum or brandy
2.5 ml (½ teaspoon) vanilla essence
2 eggs, separated
75 g (3 oz) caster sugar
284 ml (½ pint) double cream

two 23 cm (9-inch) sandwich tins, lightly greased and base-lined
a 20 cm (8-inch), round, deep cake tin, preferably loose-based
a small greaseproof paper piping bag

Whisk the egg whites for the meringue with the cream of tartar and 40 ml (2 tablespoons) of water, with an electric beater, until really stiff. Gradually whisk in the sugar and essence, whisking until the meringue is as stiff again. Gently fold in the sieved cornflour and crushed Flake, ensuring there are no dry pockets left. Divide evenly between the sandwich tins, bake in a cool oven at Gas Mark 2/150°C/300°F, on the lowest shelf, for 2 hours. Cool in the tin but first carefully loosen round the sides with a knife.

Prepare the filling. Reserve three squares of chocolate for the decoration, break up the remainder and melt it in a bowl over hot water, with the coffee, alcohol and essence. When quite smooth, cool a little before stirring into the egg yolks. Whisk the egg whites stiffly and gradually add the sugar, whisking until as stiff again. With the same whisk, whisk *half* the cream in a separate bowl, then fold into the chocolate mixture, with the egg whites.

Remove the meringue layers from the tins, ensuring the paper is peeled off, and then place one in the deep tin. Pour over the chocolate mixture and then lightly press the second meringue layer on top. Place in the freezer until set, for about 5 hours or overnight.

Melt the reserved chocolate and place in the piping bag. Whip the remaining cream so that it is spreadable. Loosen the gâteau from the sides of the tin with a hot knife round the inside, lift out carefully and place on a plate. Spread the cream over the top (and sides if you wish, depending on how uneven it is) then pipe zig-zag lines of chocolate on top. Serve fairly quickly, whilst still cold.

Serves 8–10

Craggy Chocolate Torte (page 87); Iced Meringue Marseillaise; Glossy Chocolate Gâteau

Glossy Chocolate Gâteau

This really is a very spectacular gâteau which tastes just as good as it looks. Use as much fresh fruit as possible, including fresh peaches when they are in season.

FOR THE CAKE LAYERS
50 g (2 oz) Cadbury's Bournville cocoa
125 g (4 oz) butter
225 g (8 oz) dark soft brown sugar
2 × size 2 eggs
150 g (5 oz) carton of natural yogurt
175 g (6 oz) plain flour
5 ml (1 teaspoon) baking powder
2.5 ml (½ teaspoon) bicarbonate of soda
TO COMPLETE
200 g bar of Cadbury's Bournville chocolate
1 small can of peach slices
20–40 ml (1–2 tablespoons) brandy
284 ml (½ pint) double cream
1 kiwi fruit, peeled and sliced
a few redcurrants, cherries or other fruit
chocolate leaves (page 12)

a 20 cm (8-inch), round, deep cake tin, greased and
    base-lined
a serrated cake scraper (optional)

For the cake, blend the cocoa to a paste with a little hot water. Cream the butter and sugar together really well; beat in the eggs and then the yogurt and cocoa. Fold in the sieved dry ingredients and then turn the mixture into the tin and bake at Gas Mark 5/ 190°C/375°F for about 50 minutes until cooked through. Cool in the tin before turning out.

Melt 75 g (3 oz) of the chocolate. Drain the peaches and mix the brandy into the juice. Slice the cake through the centre and soak both pieces with the peach juice mixture. Reserve 80 ml (4 tablespoons) of cream, lightly whip the remainder and then fold in the cool, melted chocolate; spread two spoonsful on to one layer of cake. Chop all but three peach slices, spread the chopped fruit over the cream filling and sandwich the cake back together. Spread the chocolate cream all over the cake, smoothing the top flat and marking round the edge with a serrated cake scraper if available.

Now make the chocolate topping by melting the remaining chocolate and stirring in the reserved cream. Leave this to cool until thick enough to coat the back of a spoon. Carefully pour the topping over the cake, encouraging it to flow attractively over the edge. Leave this to set.

Lift the gâteau on to an attractive plate, and decorate the centre with the reserved peaches, kiwi fruit and other fruit, and the chocolate leaves. If no suitable red fruit is available, brighten it up with glacé or maraschino cherries.

This gâteau needs to be kept in a cool place, preferably in the fridge.

Serves 8 generously

Meringue Cascade

A really spectacular dessert to serve your guests. The various elements of the recipe can be made in advance and the dessert assembled on the day. The fruit flavour may also be varied. As it is quite rich, a fresh fruit salad would be refreshing with this.

FOR THE MERINGUES
2 egg whites
50 g (2 oz) caster sugar
50 g (2 oz) icing sugar, sieved
30 ml (1 good tablespoon) Cadbury's Bournville cocoa

FOR THE BASE
150 g Cadbury's Bournville chocolate
1 orange
125 g (4 oz) butter
125 g (4 oz) dark, soft brown sugar
3 eggs, separated
75 g (3 oz) ground almonds
50 g (2 oz) plain flour
25 g (1 oz) Cadbury's Bournville cocoa
40 ml (2 tablespoons) Cointreau (optional)

TO COMPLETE
142 ml (¼ pint) double cream
150 g carton of mandarin yogurt
312 g can of mandarin oranges
chocolate leaves (page 12)

a large piping bag and star pipe
two baking trays covered with baking parchment
a 20 cm (8-inch), round, loose-based cake tin, greased and base-lined

For the meringues, whisk the egg whites really hard until they form stiff peaks. Gradually whisk in both the sugars until as stiff again, and then fold in the cocoa evenly. Fill the piping bag and pipe whirls of meringue about 4 cm (1½ inches) in diameter on the prepared baking trays. Bake in a very cool oven at Gas Mark ¼/ 110°C/225°F for about 1½ hours until the meringues have dried out and are crisp. Turn them over three-quarters of the way through. Cool before storing in an airtight container.

For the base, break the chocolate into a pan. Add the finely grated orange rind and strained juice. Heat slowly, stirring until the chocolate has melted. Cream the butter and sugar well together, gradually beat in the egg yolks, ground almonds and melted chocolate.

Sieve in the flour and cocoa together and stir well before folding in the whisked egg whites. Turn into the prepared tin and bake at Gas Mark 3/170°C/325°F for about 50 minutes until cooked. Cool in the tin before moistening with the Cointreau.

To complete the dessert, place the base on an attractive plate. Whip the cream and yogurt together, spread a little over the base and place the remainder in the piping bag. Pile up the meringues with the drained mandarins in between and whirls of cream. Place the chocolate leaves in position. Keep in a cool place until ready to serve.

Serves 8   *Pictured on the front cover*

Satin & Gold Celebration Cake

As the name implies, this is a cake for a special occasion. Although a sponge, it keeps well as the fondant icing prevents it drying out, so the cake can be completed several days in advance. Decorate to fit the occasion.

FOR THE CAKE
150 g Cadbury's Bournville chocolate
1 small orange
175 g (6 oz) butter
175 g (6 oz) caster or soft brown sugar
5 × size 3 eggs
75 g (3 oz) self-raising flour
5 ml (1 teaspoon) ground cinnamon
75 g (3 oz) ground almonds
50 g (2 oz) cornflour
FOR THE ALMOND PASTE
125 g (4 oz) ground almonds
125 g (4 oz) icing sugar
5 ml (1 teaspoon) ground cinnamon
1 egg yolk
100 ml (5 tablespoons) apricot jam or redcurrant
  jelly
TO COMPLETE
1 amount of chocolate fondant (page 19)
50 g bar of Cadbury's Bournville chocolate
a cake decoration of your choice
chocolate leaves (page 12)

an 18 cm (7-inch) square, deep cake tin, greased and
  base-lined
a 25 cm (10-inch) square cake board
a greaseproof paper piping bag and small star pipe

Melt the chocolate for the cake. Finely grate the orange rind and squeeze out the juice. Cream the butter and sugar together in an electric mixer if available, and then beat in the eggs with a little flour. Add the melted chocolate and then all the dry ingredients and the orange rind, with enough orange juice to make a firm dropping consistency. Turn the mixture into the tin and level the surface. Bake at Gas Mark 3/170°C/325°F for 60–70 minutes, until cooked in the centre. Cool in the tin before turning out. The cake may be stored in an airtight tin for several days at this stage, or frozen for longer.

To make the almond paste, knead the ground almonds with the sieved dry ingredients and the egg yolk, making the paste absolutely smooth. Cut the cake through the centre and then brush both cut surfaces with warm jam. Roll the almond paste to the same size as the cake, using the cake tin as a guide; trim the edges. Sandwich the cake back together with the almond paste in the centre. Brush the cake all over with the remaining jam and lift it on to the cake board.

Prepare the fondant as described. Dust the surface with cocoa and roll out the fondant large enough to cover the cake in one go. Carefully lift it on and mould the fondant over the cake, using your hands to make it smooth. Trim the edges neatly.

Melt the chocolate in a small bowl and then add the smallest drop of water (less than a quarter of a teaspoon), stirring as the chocolate thickens. Place this in the piping bag and pipe a spiral or shell edge round the base of the cake. Stick the cake decoration in position and intersperse the chocolate leaves. Add a ribbon round the edge if wished, depending on the smoothness of the fondant!

Serves 16–20

Satin & Gold Celebration Cake

Truffle Temptation Cake

With marzipan holly leaves and berries and a bright red ribbon, this makes a perfect adult Christmas cake.

FOR THE CAKE
250 g (9 oz) slightly salted butter
250 g (9 oz) dark soft brown sugar
4 × size 2 or 3 eggs
20 ml (1 tablespoon) golden syrup or honey
150 g (5 oz) carton of natural yogurt
250 g (9 oz) self-raising flour
40 g (1½ oz) Cadbury's Bournville cocoa
40 g (1½ oz) ground almonds or hazelnuts
FOR THE SYRUP
125 g (4 oz) caster sugar
125 ml (¼ pint) water
80 ml (4 tablespoons) dark rum
FOR THE FILLING AND ICING
80 ml (4 tablespoons) cranberry or redcurrant jelly
200 g bar of Cadbury's Bournville chocolate
284 ml (½ pint) double cream
20–40 ml (1–2 tablespoons) rum
FOR THE TRUFFLES AND DECORATION
100 g bar of Cadbury's Bournville chocolate
25 g (1 oz) slightly salted butter
60 ml (3 tablespoons) cream from the icing
25 g (1 oz) ground almonds
50 g (2 oz) icing sugar
75 g (3 oz) sweet biscuits, crushed
40 ml (2 tablespoons) rum
50 g (2 oz) glacé cherries dusted in sugar
chocolate leaves (page 12)

*a 25 cm (10-inch), round cake tin, preferably
   loose-based, greased and base-lined*

Make the cake by creaming the butter and sugar together. Gradually beat in the eggs, syrup or honey and yogurt and when well mixed, fold in the sieved flour and cocoa, and then the nuts. Spread the mixture in the tin, hollow out the centre slightly, and bake at Gas Mark 4/180°C/350°F for about 1 hour until cooked.

Slowly dissolve the sugar in the water in a pan and then boil briefly to thicken the syrup a little. Cool before adding the rum, and then moisten the warm cake whilst still in the tin. Leave to cool completely before turning out.

Split the cake in half and sandwich it back together with the jelly. Melt the broken-up chocolate with all but 60 ml (3 tablespoons) of cream. When smooth, whisk together. Add the rum. Leave the icing to cool and thicken before spreading it over the cake; place the cake on the serving plate first if you are brave enough! Otherwise, ice it on a board and transfer when set. Make the surface quite smooth.

Now make the truffles by melting 75 g (3 oz) of the chocolate and grating the remainder. Stir all the ingredients into the melted chocolate, mixing well. Leave in the fridge until firm enough to handle fairly easily. Divide the mixture evenly and roll into about 18 balls, tossing them in the grated chocolate. Leave in the fridge until firm.

Decorate the cake with some truffles, frosted cherries and chocolate leaves. Keep cool until required.

Serves about 10

Note: The truffles can also be made on their own.

Truffle Temptation Cake

Time for Treats

Nothing complicated here, because these recipes mainly use store-cupboard ingredients, and just need a good stir before they are pressed into a tin. Older children will enjoy making them and even the younger members of the family could be introduced to the joys of cooking with these quick and easy recipes. Try the Magic Flake Cake for a particularly moist cake with an unusual texture.

Peanut Squares

225 g (8 oz) Rich Tea biscuits, or use a variety from the biscuit tin
125 g (4 oz) unsalted butter
225 g (8 oz) crunchy peanut butter
50 g (2 oz) glacé cherries, quartered
FOR THE ICING
200 g bar of Cadbury's Bournville chocolate
10 ml (2 teaspoons) flavourless oil
50 g (2 oz) caster sugar
80 ml (4 tablespoons) water

an 18 × 28 cm (7 × 11 inch), shallow cake tin, greased

Crush the biscuits, leaving them a bit crunchy if you prefer. Slowly melt the butter and then stir in the biscuits, peanut butter and cherries. Press the mixture into the tin and then chill to harden.

Break up the chocolate and melt it in a pan with the other icing ingredients, stirring until quite smooth. Beat to obtain a good consistency, then pour the icing over the base and leave in a cold place to set. Cut into 18 squares before lifting out.

Tip: Using crumbs from the biscuit tin gives a different flavour each time you make these.

Makes 18

Mocha Chocolate Drink

425 ml (¾ pint) milk
30 ml (1 good tablespoon) Cadbury's Bournville cocoa, plus a little extra
5 ml (1 teaspoon) dry instant coffee
40 ml (2 tablespoons) icing sugar
40 ml (2 tablespoons) whipped cream

Whisk the milk with the cocoa, coffee and sugar whilst heating to boiling point. Pour into cups or mugs, top with the whipped cream and sprinkle with extra cocoa.

Serves 2

Triple Slices; Split-level Oaties; Peanut Squares

Split-Level Oaties

175 g (6 oz) stoned dates
75 g (3 oz) glacé cherries
25 g (1 oz) raisins
finely grated rind and juice of 1 lemon
120 ml (6 tablespoons) water
225 g (8 oz) margarine
225 g (8 oz) wholemeal flour
225 g (8 oz) rolled oats
75 g (3 oz) soft brown sugar
25 g (1 oz) Cadbury's Bournville chocolate
a Cadbury's Flake family box

an 18 × 28 cm (7 × 11 inch) cake tin, greased
   lightly

Chop the fruit and place it in a pan with the finely grated lemon rind, juice and water. Bring to the boil and simmer gently for a few minutes until the fruit is soft, then cool.

Rub the margarine into the flour and then mix in the oats and sugar. Press half this mixture into the tin, spread over the fruit and cover with remaining dry mixture, pressing it on lightly. Bake at Gas Mark 4/ 180°C/350°F for about 40 minutes until lightly browned. Cut into 16 fingers and leave in the tin until cold.

Lift out and spread a little chocolate or jam on 16 Flake, then stick them on to the oaties.

Makes 16

Triple Slices

Tray bakes are always popular and this one is particularly easy to make. The Buttons on top give a lovely flavour.

225 g (8 oz) butter or margarine
200 g (7 oz) digestive-type biscuits
150 g Cadbury's Bournville chocolate
50 g (2 oz) soft brown sugar
50 g (2 oz) caster sugar
150 g (5 oz) self-raising flour
125 ml (¼ pint) milk
2 packets of Cadbury's creamy-white Buttons
a little jam

an 18 × 28 cm (7 × 11 inch), deep swiss roll tin,
   greased

Melt half the fat, crush the biscuits and stir in. Press the biscuit crust into the tin and then chill.

Melt the chocolate, beat the remaining fat with both sugars until really smooth, gradually beat in the melted chocolate, flour and milk, making a dropping consistency. Fold in the contents of one packet of Buttons and then spread over the biscuit crust. Bake at Gas Mark 5/190°C/375°F for about 35 minutes. Cool in the tin.

Cut in half lengthways and then into 16 slices. Place three Buttons on each slice, securing them with a little jam.

Makes 16

Button Drops

A batch of these are always useful, but keep them airtight as they go soft.

100 g bar of Cadbury's Bournville chocolate
225 g (8 oz) soft margarine
50 g (2 oz) icing sugar
2.5 ml (½ teaspoon) vanilla essence
40 ml (2 tablespoons) milk
225 g (8 oz) plain flour
125 g (4 oz) cornflour
2.5 ml (½ teaspoon) baking powder
a packet of Cadbury's creamy-white chocolate
   Buttons

a large piping bag with star nozzle
2 baking trays, greased lightly

Melt the chocolate. Cream the margarine and sugar together until very pale in colour, then add the melted chocolate, essence and milk. Beat in the dry ingredients and continue to beat until the mixture is fairly soft. Fill the piping bag and pipe about 30 biscuits on to the trays, allowing room for them to spread. Bake at Gas Mark 5/190°C/375°F for about 15 minutes.

Immediately they come out of the oven, press a Button into the centre of each biscuit. Leave to cool and harden before removing from the trays. Store in an airtight container.

Makes about 30

Kaleidoscope Krisp

This is a favourite with the younger children. Use Cadbury's Buttons when Mini Eggs are not available.

200 g bar of Cadbury's Dairy Milk milk chocolate
50 g (2 oz) soft margarine
50 g (2 oz) desiccated coconut
25 g (1 oz) crisped rice cereal
a packet of Cadbury's Mini Eggs
TO DECORATE
125 g (4 oz) icing sugar
pink and blue food colouring

a 20 cm (8-inch), round, loose-based cake tin

Melt the chocolate. Add the margarine, coconut and cereal and stir well until completely coated. Press the mixture into the tin lightly. Press the Mini Eggs in at regular intervals around the side. Leave to set hard.

Cut into 12 even-sized wedges before decorating with icing. Sieve the icing sugar into a bowl and add enough water, lemon juice or orange juice to give a fairly thick coating consistency. Divide the icing into three, colouring one portion pink, another blue and leaving the third white. Pipe or drizzle the icings in zig-zags in alternate colours over each triangle. Leave to set.

Makes 12

Flapjacks

250 g (9 oz) margarine or butter
75 g (3 oz) light soft brown sugar
40 ml (2 tablespoons) golden syrup
100 g bar of Cadbury's Bournville chocolate
325 g (11 oz) rolled oats
150 g (5 oz) stoned dates, chopped

a 23 × 33 cm (9 × 13-inch) swiss roll tin, greased
**   lightly**

Melt the margarine, sugar and syrup with the broken-up chocolate in a pan over a gentle heat. When liquid, stir in the oats and dates, then spread the mixture evenly in the tin. Bake at Gas Mark 4/180°C/350°F for 40–45 minutes. Cool slightly before cutting down the centre, then across, into 18 finger shapes.

Makes 18

Button Drops; Flapjacks; Kaleidoscope Crisp

Choco-Cherry Ice Block

100 g bar of Cadbury's Bournville chocolate
200 g (7 oz) sweetened condensed milk
10 ml (2 teaspoons) cherry brandy
284 ml (½ pint) whipping cream
397 g (14 oz) can of cherry pie filling
2 extra squares of chocolate, to decorate

a 1 kg (2 lb) loaf tin, greased and strip-lined
a small greaseproof paper piping bag

Break the chocolate into a bowl standing over a pan of hot but not boiling water. Add the condensed milk and stir occasionally until the chocolate has melted and the mixture thickens, which will take about 10 minutes. Take off the heat and stir in 160 ml (8 tablespoons) water, with the cherry brandy. Beat vigorously. Chill in the refrigerator.

Lightly whip the cream and fold it into the chilled mixture. Pour into a suitable container, preferably metal for speed, then freeze until partially frozen.

Now turn the ice cream into a bowl and whisk until smooth. Place half the cherry pie filling straight into the loaf tin and stir the remainder through the ice cream. Pour into the loaf tin and freeze overnight. Wrap and label if to be kept longer. Use within 6–8 weeks.

Dip the tin in hot water just enough to loosen the sides before turning the ice cream on to a plate. Melt the two squares of chocolate, fill the piping bag and then pipe lines at an angle over the top. Serve in slices.

Serves 6

Square Deals

150 g Cadbury's Bournville chocolate
25 g (1 oz) golden syrup
50 g (2 oz) butter
175 g (6 oz) digestive biscuits
25 g (1 oz) glacé cherries
50 g (2 oz) dried apricots
50 g (2 oz) walnuts, chopped
FOR THE ICING
50 g (2 oz) butter
20 ml (1 tablespoon) milk
125 g (4 oz) icing sugar

an 18 cm (7-inch) square tin, greased lightly

Melt 100 g of the chocolate with the syrup and butter, stirring until smooth. Crush the biscuits quite roughly, and then stir in, with the chopped fruit and half the nuts. Press the mixture into the prepared tin and leave to set.

Melt the remaining 50 g of chocolate with the butter and then cool slightly before adding the milk. Add the sieved icing sugar, beating hard until the icing thickens. Swirl it over the biscuit mixture, sprinkle over the remaining nuts and leave in a cool place to set. Later carefully cut into nine squares.

Makes 9

Magic Flake Cake

350 g (12 oz) plain cake crumbs
4 × size 2 eggs, separated
5 ml (1 teaspoon) vanilla essence
40 ml (2 tablespoons) rum
50 g bar of Cadbury's Bournville chocolate
75 g (3 oz) blanched almonds
6 Cadbury's Flake from the family box
175 g (6 oz) caster sugar
TO COMPLETE
426 ml (¾ pint) double cream
80 ml (4 tablespoons) icing sugar, sieved
40 ml (2 tablespoons) rum
4 Cadbury's Flake from the family box

a 20 cm (8-inch), round, deep cake tin, greased and
*   base-lined*
a piping bag and star pipe

Work the cake crumbs in a food processor or blender so that they are quite fine. Whisk the egg yolks, essence and rum together well until pale in colour. Fold in the cake crumbs, grated chocolate, chopped nuts and crumbled Flake. Whisk the egg whites stiffly, add the sugar and continue whisking until as stiff again. Fold both mixtures together then turn into the tin and level the top. Bake at Gas Mark 4/180°C/350°F for about 1 hour 10 minutes, until cooked through. Leave briefly before turning out to cool.

Slice the cake evenly into three. Whip the cream, sieved icing sugar and rum together until stiff enough to spread. Put some into the piping bag, and sandwich the cake back together with the remaining cream, also covering the top. Pipe 8 whirls of cream, stick half a Flake into each and lift the cake on to a plate.

Serves 8 generously

No-Bake Chocolate Triangles

200 g bar of Cadbury's Bournville chocolate
150 g (5 oz) butter
1 egg
25 g (1 oz) caster sugar
225 g (8 oz) ginger biscuits
50 g (2 oz) stem ginger
icing sugar
225 g (8 oz) kumquats (optional)
550 ml (1 pint) orange juice (optional)

a 20 cm (8-inch), round, loose-based cake tin, lightly
*   greased and base-lined*

Gently melt the chocolate and butter together and then beat in the egg and sugar. Crush the biscuits quite coarsely and chop the ginger; stir them into the chocolate mixture. Pour into the tin and leave in a cool place overnight to set. Cut into eight even wedges. Dust with icing sugar.

If you like, stew the kumquats in the orange juice mixed with some of the ginger syrup for about 25 minutes, until soft. Leave to cool and then serve with the Chocolate Triangles: the sharp contrast of flavours makes this extra effort worthwhile.

Makes 8

Magic Flake Cake

Plan a Party

Children of all ages love a party – especially their own! Birthday parties are, of course, the most popular, but there are plenty of other occasions: Christmas, Guy Fawkes Night, Hallowe'en, Valentine's Day. Why not break up the summer holiday with a picnic or barbecue?

Exciting parties, especially those for younger children don't just happen: they need to be planned well in advance so that everyone, including you, can enjoy themselves. The secret of success is not to be too ambitious: take account of your house and garden size, plus your own culinary talents, and do consider the costs. Simple ideas are often most successful.

The birthday cake is undoubtedly one of the highlights of the party and it has to be something different every year! In this chapter you will find ideas for spectacular birthday cakes which are easy to make.

Choose your party food carefully. Avoid very rich and sticky things and don't be surprised if the young ones eat very little. Allow 4–6 savoury items, including crisps, cheese snacks or sausages, plus two sweet items, ice-cream and jelly. Older children will prefer more savoury items and, whatever the age, have plenty of soft drinks as any party activity works up a thirst!

Banana Cream Pie

125 g (4 oz) caster sugar
40 ml (2 tablespoons) cornflour
2 eggs
275 ml (½ pint) milk
150 g Cadbury's Bournville chocolate
50 g (2 oz) butter
2.5 ml (½ teaspoon) vanilla essence
1 ripe banana
284 ml (½ pint) whipping cream
a 20 cm (8-inch) cooked shortcrust pastry case (page 23)
FOR THE TOPPING
142 ml (¼ pint) double cream (optional)
150 g (5 oz) carton of yogurt
20 ml (1 tablespoon) icing sugar (optional)
1 banana, sliced and dipped in lemon juice

Mix the sugar, cornflour and eggs to a custard. Heat slowly with the milk, stirring without boiling. When thickened, take off the heat.

Make some chocolate curls for the decoration; melt the remaining chocolate in the custard. Stir in the butter, essence, mashed banana and lightly whipped cream. When cool, pour into the flan case and refrigerate until lightly set.

Whip the cream (if using), yogurt and icing sugar together. Fold in the sliced banana, then pile on to the flan. Top with chocolate curls.

Tip: Use either a plain or a chocolate pastry case.

Serves 8

Friendly Ghost; Monkey Face Biscuits (page 114)

Friendly Ghost

It really is necessary to make the icing over hot water to get the right consistency and lovely, shiny appearance. Keep beating if in doubt. A rotary beater can also be used but it is hard work!

FOR THE CAKE
225 g (8 oz) soft margarine
225 g (8 oz) caster sugar
4 eggs
225 g (8 oz) self-raising flour, sieved
10 ml (2 teaspoons) Cadbury's Bournville cocoa
pink food colouring
80 ml (4 tablespoons) jam
FOR THE FROSTING AND DECORATION
2 egg whites
350 g (12 oz) icing sugar, sieved
a pinch of cream of tartar
80 ml (4 tablespoons) water
1 packet of Cadbury's milk chocolate Buttons
2 Bassett's Allsorts pink coconut wheels

an 18 × 28 cm (7 × 11 inch) square cake tin, greased and base-lined

---

Cream together the margarine and sugar until light and fluffy. Slowly beat in the eggs, and fold in the flour. Divide the cake mixture into three equal portions. Mix the cocoa to a paste with boiling water and then stir into one amount; stir a few drops of pink colouring into the second portion and leave the third plain. Place alternate coloured spoonsful of mixture in the tin, smoothing it over with a spatula. Bake at Gas Mark 4/180°C/350°F for 30–40 minutes. Carefully turn out and cool.

Cut a semi-circular piece off the cake approxi-mately 2.5 cm (1 inch) from the top of a shorter side (Fig. 1). Slice the 'cut-off' corners in half down the middle (Fig. 2) and position halfway down the sides to represent up-held arms (Fig. 3).

For the frosting, place the egg whites, icing sugar, cream of tartar and water in a bowl and whisk over a pan of hot water until the icing is satin-smooth and white, which will take a good 10 minutes with a hand-held electric mixer.

Swirl the frosting over the cake. Polish the Buttons with your fingers to make them shine and use to make the 'eyes', then a 'smiling mouth' as shown in the photograph. Place the liquorice sweets in the centre of the eyes to glow.

Serves 8–12

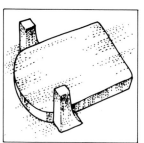

Fig. 1 *Cut off a piece for 'arms'* Fig. 2 *Halve it.* Fig. 3 *Position the 'arms'*

Crazy Paving

FOR THE CAKE
a 300 g packet of plain sweet biscuits
200 g bar of Cadbury's Bournville chocolate
125 g (4 oz) butter
10 ml (2 teaspoons) Cadbury's Bournville cocoa
125 g (4 oz) icing sugar
1 egg
60 ml (3 tablespoons) cherry brandy
75 g (3 oz) glacé cherries, halved
FOR THE ICING AND DECORATION
100 g bar of Cadbury's Bournville chocolate
25 g (1 oz) butter
125 g (4 oz) icing sugar
20 ml (1 tablespoon) Cadbury's Bournville cocoa
5 glacé cherries, halved
a few flaked almonds, browned

a large sheet of greaseproof paper

Break up the biscuits and crush them, ensuring they are not too fine. Melt the chocolate, then cool. Beat together the butter, cocoa, icing sugar and egg, and when well creamed, beat in the liqueur; it may begin to curdle but will revert to normal as the chocolate is now stirred in. Add the cherries and biscuits, stirring it all together well. Turn on to the greaseproof paper and form into a roll measuring 5–6 cm (a good 2 inches) in diameter and about 30 cm (12 inches) long. Wrap firmly and then leave in a refrigerator overnight.

Make the icing by melting the broken-up chocolate with the butter and 40 ml (2 tablespoons) of water; beat in the icing sugar and cocoa. Cool as you beat so that it is thick enough to pour over the biscuit roll.

Unwrap the biscuit roll and place on a long plate or board. Pour over the icing and decorate with halved cherries and the almonds. Cut into slices.

Tip: Cut the roll into slices and put each one in a paper cake case – saves crumbs all over the place!

Serves about 10

Easy Chocolate Ice Cream

150 g Cadbury's Bournville chocolate
397 g (14 oz) can of sweetened condensed milk
5 ml (1 teaspoon) vanilla or sweet orange essence
568 ml (1 pint) double cream, whipped

Break the chocolate into a pan with the condensed milk and stir over a gentle heat until melted. Stir in 120 ml (6 tablespoons) water (or orange juice) and the essence. Fold in the whipped cream and then turn into a suitable container and freeze.

In the normal way, stir and beat the mixture occasionally before it gets too hard; or make the ice cream in an ice cream maker. Freeze for at least 24 hours to harden completely.

Serves 6–8

Stockade Cake

No special tins are required for this cake; though a hexagonal tin could be used, this doesn't create 'turrets'. I made this originally for my son and it was a big hit. Each child took home a soldier, cowboy or Indian as well as a gooey piece of cake!

225 g (8 oz) soft margarine
225 g (8 oz) caster sugar
4 eggs
200 g (7 oz) self-raising flour
2.5 ml (½ teaspoon) baking powder
1 orange
25 g (1 oz) Cadbury's Bournville cocoa
TO DECORATE
675 g (1½ lb) Chocolate Butter Icing (page 20)
a Cadbury's Flake family box
soft brown sugar

toy soldiers, cowboys and Indians
candles and holders
an 8 cm (3¼-inch) diameter, clean, empty food tin
a 23 cm (9-inch) square cake tin, greased and
*   base-lined*
a baking tray
a 30 cm (12-inch) cake or chopping board.

To make the special shape, place the food tin, wrapped with greaseproof paper or foil, in the centre of the cake tin. Weight it down with scale weights or something similar. This makes the hole in the centre of the cake.

With an electric mixer, beat the margarine and sugar together well. Gradually beat in the eggs with a little flour and then fold in the sieved flour and baking powder. Halve the mixture; add the finely grated orange rind and half the juice to one amount, the cocoa and remaining juice to the other. Place alternate spoonfuls of both mixtures in the prepared tin and smooth over the surface, being careful not to disturb the colours too much. Bake on a baking tray at Gas Mark 4/180°C/350°F for about 50 minutes until well risen and cooked through in the centre. Leave for a few minutes before carefully turning out, removing the tin in the centre first. Cool the cake.

Have the chocolate butter icing made before you assemble the cake. Measure 7.5 cm (3 inches) in from each corner and mark the line across so that you make a straight clean cut, cutting a triangular piece off each corner (Fig. 1). Make sure this is done accurately. Lift the cake on to the board and then stick the triangular 'turrets' upright on each side with a little butter icing (Fig. 2). Spread the whole cake with a very little icing and do not worry if the crumbs get mixed in. Chill for ½ hour or place in the freezer until the surface is hard enough to spread the remaining butter icing on top.

Now the crumbs will not get into the icing nearly so easily. Begin with the hole in the centre and cover the whole cake neatly. Stand one Flake upright at either side to make an entrance in the middle of one side of

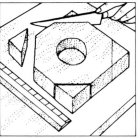

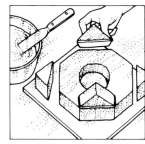

Fig. 1   Fig 2.

Stockade Cake

the cake. Split the remaining Flake lengthways into thinner pieces and press these on to the outer edge of the cake; it is a fiddly job but it does look effective. Scatter brown sugar round about for 'sand' and arrange the soldiers, cowboys and Indians. Lastly arrange the correct number of candles in position.

Serves 12–20

Flake Away Island

Adapt the theme to whatever you choose – a zoo visit, holiday cake, Treasure Island or just a fairy-tale island; this must be one of the most adaptable ideas ever.

675 g (1½ lb) cake (about a 3-egg creamed mixture)
675 g (1½ lb) Vanilla Butter Icing (page 20)
60 ml (3 tablespoons) lemon curd
green food colouring
12 Cadbury's Flake from the family box
40 ml (2 tablespoons) demerara sugar
50 g (2 oz) light soft brown sugar
20 ml (1 tablespoon) desiccated coconut
cake decorations for the chosen theme

a 30 cm (12-inch) cake board

Break up the cake. Work the butter icing so that it is not too hard and beat in the lemon curd. Stick the cake together with some of the icing and form it into an island shape straight on the cake board. Make a few hillocks too. Soften the butter icing by adding a tablespoon or two of hot water as necessary so that it can easily be spread all over the cake.

Carefully cut the Flake into thin pieces the depth of the cake and then press them on to the cake sides, to represent a rocky coastline. Make a cove. Sprinkle the top with the demerara sugar and any Flake crumbs. Spread the soft brown sugar round the bottom edge of the cake as 'sand'. Rub green food colouring into the coconut and make small patches of green on the 'island' surface.

Finally add decorations for your chosen theme, e.g. use small pieces of palm, a small treasure chest and Cadbury's Buttons for treasure. Buttons also make excellent stepping-stones. Let your imagination run riot!

Gingery Chocolate Slice

a 200 g packet of ginger biscuits
200 g (7 oz) can of pineapple pieces
200 g bar Cadbury's Bournville chocolate
175 g (6 oz) unsalted butter
25 g (1 oz) ground almonds
75 g (3 oz) glacé cherries, chopped

a ½ kg (1 lb) loaf tin, lightly greased and base-lined

Crush the biscuits quite roughly. Drain off the liquid, reserve 10 pieces of pineapple and then chop the remainder in half. Break up the chocolate and melt it with the butter in a bowl over a gentle heat, or in a microwave on DEFROST for 7 minutes. Stir in the biscuits, ground almonds, chopped cherries and pine-apple, mixing thoroughly.

Arrange the reserved pineapple attractively in the base of the tin and then evenly press in the chocolate mixture. Cover and refrigerate for at least 4 hours, or preferably overnight to harden properly. Serve in thick slices because of the chunky texture.

Serves 6

Flake Away Island

Monkey Face Biscuits

These cheeky-faced biscuits go down well with small boys, who like to choose the naughtiest!

125 g (4 oz) butter
125 g (4 oz) caster sugar
1 egg
2.5 ml (½ teaspoon) vanilla essence
300 g (10 oz) plain flour
75 g (3 oz) Cadbury's Bournvita
TO DECORATE
150 g Cadbury's Bournville chocolate
5 ml (1 teaspoon) flavourless oil
4 Cadbury's Flake
a large packet of Cadbury's milk chocolate Buttons

a 7.5 cm (3-inch) plain cutter
a baking tray, floured lightly
a greaseproof paper piping bag
paper hats (optional)

Cream the butter and sugar together well and then beat in the egg and essence. Add the flour and Bournvita, and bind the biscuit dough together. Knead on a lightly floured surface until smooth. Roll out, not too thinly and cut out the biscuits, re-rolling the scraps in between. Place on the lightly floured baking tray and bake at Gas Mark 5/190°C/375°F for 12–15 minutes until lightly browned and cooked. Leave to cool before removing.

Melt the chocolate with the oil. Carefully dip one end of each biscuit into the chocolate icing and then fill the piping bag with the remainder. Sprinkle on crumbs of Flake for 'hair'. Rub the Buttons a little so they shine and then stick them on with the icing as 'cauliflower ears'. Pipe a variety of faces as illustrated, using simple lines. Leave to set.

Triangular coloured paper hats may be popped over the 'hair', with names written on them for each guest.

Makes about 20   *Pictured on page 107*

Swirling Mist

25 g (1 oz) Cadbury's Bournville cocoa
25 g (1 oz) cornflour
125 g (4 oz) caster sugar
568 ml (1 pint) milk
14 g (½ oz) gelatine
2 ripe bananas
142 ml (¼ pint) natural or flavoured yogurt
142 ml (¼ pint) whipping cream

a wide glass bowl

Blend the cocoa, cornflour and sugar into a paste with a little milk taken from the measured amount. Heat the remaining milk then whisk it into the cocoa mixture. Return to the heat, stirring as it boils. Sprinkle the gelatine on to very hot water and stir until dissolved. When cool, stir into the cooling sauce, with the mashed bananas. Whip the yogurt and cream together until thick, swirl through the chocolate mixture and pour it all into the bowl. Chill overnight.

Serves 6–8

Cracker Cake

Although this is appropriate at Christmas time, there are many other occasions throughout the year when this cake could be used, for example birthdays, with the name written on top. Contrasting piping looks spectacular and you could really go to town decorating the cracker with pieces of net and ribbon.

FOR THE CAKE
2 eggs
50 g (2 oz) caster sugar
50 g (2 oz) plain flour
20 ml (1 tablespoon) Cadbury's Bournville cocoa
FOR THE FILLING
50 g bar of Cadbury's Bournville chocolate
40 g (1½ oz) butter
75 g (3 oz) icing sugar, sieved
2 Cadbury's Flake
40 ml (2 tablespoons) jam
FOR THE FONDANT AND DECORATION
350 g (12 oz) icing sugar
60 ml (3 tablespoons) Cadbury's Bournville cocoa
50 g (2 oz) liquid glucose
1 egg white
a packet of Cadbury's milk chocolate Buttons
a packet of Cadbury's creamy-white Buttons

an 18 × 28 cm (7 × 11 inch) swiss roll tin,
*   greased and lined*
greaseproof paper
crêpe paper and ribbon
a Christmas cake decoration

Whisk the eggs and sugar for the cake in a bowl over a pan of hot water, or use an electric mixer. Whisk hard until thick enough to leave a definite trail, which will take about 10 minutes. Sieve the flour and cocoa together and then carefully fold in with a tablespoon of warm water, ensuring no pockets of flour are left. Turn the mixture into the prepared tin and level the surface by tilting the tin; do not spread. Bake in a fairly hot oven, Gas Mark 6/200°C/400°F, for about 12 minutes.

Dust a large sheet of greaseproof paper with caster sugar. Turn the swiss roll on to this and carefully peel off the lining paper. Trim the cake edges and then roll up with the paper inside. Cool on a wire tray.

Melt the chocolate for the filling. Cream the butter and sieved icing sugar together until soft, and then add the cooled melted chocolate. Carefully unroll the swiss roll and then spread it with chocolate icing. Lay the Flake end-to-end across the short side, allowing them to protrude at the edges, and then roll up tightly. Brush the cake with warmed jam.

Sieve the icing sugar and cocoa for the fondant into a bowl and make a well in the centre. Add the liquid glucose and egg white, working it with a wooden spoon to bind the fondant together. Dust the surface with sifted cocoa, and then roll the fondant into an oblong large enough to cover the swiss roll, pressing it into place. Neaten the ends but keep the Flake protruding. Rub the Buttons between your fingers to make them shine and then stick them on at either end, alternating the white and milk chocolate Buttons. Use jam if necessary to secure them. Make a cracker frill for each end with the crêpe paper and tie securely round the Flake. Complete with a Christmas decoration in the centre of the cake. Lift on to a cake board.

Serves about 6

Kite Cake

This cake is easily transported.

FOR THE CAKE
75 g (3 oz) soft margarine
75 g (3 oz) soft brown sugar
200 g (7 oz) self-raising flour
2.5 ml (½ teaspoon) bicarbonate of soda
60 g (a good 2 oz) Cadbury's drinking chocolate
2 × size 2 eggs
2 large ripe bananas
FOR THE FROSTING
125 g (4 oz) slightly salted butter
20 ml (1 tablespoon) Cadbury's Bournvita
100 ml (5 tablespoons) milk
400 g (14 oz) icing sugar
60 ml (3 tablespoons) Cadbury's drinking chocolate
TO DECORATE
a packet each of Cadbury's milk chocolate and
    creamy-white Buttons
3 Cadbury's Flake
1 glacé cherry

an 18 × 28 cm (7 × 11 inch), cake tin, greased and
    base-lined
an 18 cm (11-inch) square cake board
1 metre bright ribbon, or crêpe paper strips
birthday candles and holders (optional)

Put all the cake ingredients in a bowl and mash together with a potato masher or fork. Make sure there are no lumps remaining before spreading evenly in the tin. Bake at Gas Mark 4/180°C/350°F for about 40 minutes until cooked. Turn out and cool.

Melt the butter and Bournvita in the milk for the frosting; cool before beating in 350 g (12 oz) only of the icing sugar, making it smooth and glossy. Divide the frosting in half; add the drinking chocolate to one amount and the remaining icing sugar to the other, then beat both again. Adjust the texture as necessary by adding a little more milk or icing sugar.

Cut the cake in half diagonally (Fig. 1) and then turn one piece over and lay it next to the other piece, the other way round, making a kite shape (Fig. 2). Sandwich the two pieces together with a little frosting. Mark a line across the widest part of the cake and then spread alternate colours of frosting in the triangles. Put lines of halved Buttons where the colours meet and then press white ones on to the darker chocolate frosting and vice versa. Press crushed Flake round the edges and lift the cake on to the cake board. Place the cherry on top. Make a kite tail from the ribbon or paper. For a birthday party, arrange the holders and birthday candles on top.

Serves about 12

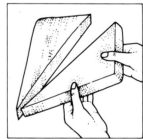
Fig. 1

Fig 2.

Kite Cake; Cracker Cake

Microwave Magic

Chocolate cakes were early favourites for the microwave method of cooking because of their rich colour. The recipes have been modified in this chapter so that you will find that they contain extra moisture and are more 'batter-like'. They are therefore not easily adaptable to more conventional methods of cooking. The selection chosen have both good texture and taste and are easily prepared.

Please refer to the manufacturer's instructions for your own model of microwave cooker, as terminology differs. The recipes were tested on a 650-watt model and recipes will need to be adjusted: for a lower wattage of 500 watts, add about 20 seconds for every minute and for a 600-watt model, add about 15 seconds for every minute. Standing time is important and should be counted *after* the times given in the recipes, as the food continues to cook by natural conduction, achieving a perfect result and avoiding the all-too-often 'dry' texture of some microwaved recipes. This is particularly important in chocolate recipes, which should be moist and luscious.

Melting chocolate in a microwave is excellent. We advise DEFROST as being the most suitable, after exhaustive tests. The bar can be left whole or broken up in to a bowl; place it in the cooker and heat on the DEFROST setting for 4 minutes. Again, the standing time is necessary, so leave the chocolate until it has softened right through before stirring it gently. Exact timing for recipes is important, so follow the instructions and enjoy the results!

Refer to your manufacturer's instruction book for exact microwave settings, but as a guide, these are general comparisons:

HIGH 100%   SIMMER 50%   WARM 10–20%
REHEAT 70–90%   DEFROST 30%

Coconut Bars

a small can of condensed milk
125 g (4 oz) margarine
finely grated rind of 1 lemon
225 g (8 oz) digestive biscuits, crushed roughly
75 g (3 oz) desiccated coconut
200 g bar of Cadbury's Dairy Milk milk chocolate or Bournville chocolate

a 18 × 28 cm (7 × 11 inch) cake tin, greased lightly

Microwave the condensed milk and margarine in a bowl on HIGH for 3 minutes, and then stir in the lemon rind, biscuits and coconut. Carefully press the mixture into the tin and chill for about an hour.

Break the chocolate into a bowl and melt on DEFROST for 3 minutes and then leave to melt completely. Spread the chocolate over the base and mark into shapes with a fork. When set, cut into 16 finger shapes.

Makes 16   *Pictured on the back cover*

Butterscotch Fudge Cake; Dreamy Chocolate Pie (page 122)

Butterscotch Fudge Cake

FOR THE CAKE
100 g bar of Cadbury's Bournville chocolate
60 ml (2 fl oz) oil
180 ml (6 fl oz) water
125 g (4 oz) margarine
225 g (8 oz) caster sugar
300 g (10 oz) self-raising flour
2 eggs
120 ml (4 fl oz) milk
5 ml (1 teaspoon) vanilla essence
5 ml (1 teaspoon) bicarbonate of soda
FOR THE FROSTING
175 g (6 oz) butter
175 g (6 oz) soft brown sugar
80 ml (4 tablespoons) milk
5 ml (1 teaspoon) vanilla or rum essence
500 g (1 lb 2 oz) icing sugar, sieved

a 20 cm (8-inch), round, microwave-proof dish at least 7.5 cm (3 inches) deep, greased and base-lined

Break the chocolate into a bowl with the oil, water and margarine, and then microwave on HIGH for 4 minutes. Beat in the remaining cake ingredients until the mixture is smooth. Turn into the prepared dish and microwave on SIMMER for 16–17 minutes until cooked and well risen, turning occasionally. Leave to stand for 10 minutes before turning out on to a wire tray covered with cling film. Turn the right way up again before leaving to cool completely.

For the frosting, melt the butter with the sugar in a bowl on HIGH for 3 minutes, stirring well after every minute. Stir in the milk and essence, then microwave for a further 2 minutes. Beat in the sieved icing sugar and continue beating until the frosting has cooled and thickened; it will go quite thick. Slice the cake in half and sandwich it back together with about three tablespoons of the icing spread in between. Carefully cover the cake completely with the remaining icing, swirling it attractively with a palette knife. Lift on to a plate or board ready to eat. The icing will get a slight crust as it sets. *Serves 8*

Fast Fudge

150 g Cadbury's Bournville chocolate
125 g (4 oz) butter
80 ml (4 tablespoons) orange juice
450 g (1 lb) icing sugar
75 g (3 oz) glacé cherries, chopped

an 18 cm (7-inch) square container, greased

Break the chocolate into a bowl and then melt with the butter and orange juice on DEFROST for 4 minutes. Stir until smooth and then sieve in the icing sugar and beat until really smooth and thickened. Beat in two-thirds of the cherries before pouring into the container to set in the fridge overnight.

Cut into 36 squares and decorate with the remaining pieces of cherry. Keep chilled.

Criss-Cross Sponge Pudding

411 g (14½ oz) can of black or red cherries in syrup
5 ml (1 teaspoon) cornflour
150 g Cadbury's Bournville chocolate
80 ml (4 tablespoons) bland vegetable oil
50 g (2 oz) margarine
125 g (4 oz) caster sugar
150 g (5 oz) self-raising flour
1 × size 2 egg
60 ml (3 tablespoons) milk
2.5 ml (½ teaspoon) vanilla essence
50 g (2 oz) marzipan

a 1.1-litre (2-pint) microwave-proof dish

Drain and pit the cherries and then place the fruit in the dish. Blend the cornflour with the fruit syrup and microwave on HIGH for 3 minutes, whisking well each minute. Pour this over the cherries.

Grate 50 g of the chocolate and then melt the remaining chocolate with the oil, 80 ml (4 tablespoons) of water and the margarine on HIGH for 4 minutes. Whisk until smooth. Omitting the marzipan, gradually whisk in the remaining ingredients and then pour into the dish. Sprinkle with the grated chocolate.

Microwave on HIGH for 7 minutes. Roll out the marzipan quite thinly and then cut it into narrow strips. Twist these and arrange them in a criss-cross pattern over the pudding. Cook for a further 7 minutes. Serve warm with Chocolate Custard (page 18) or single cream.

Serves 6   *Pictured on page 125*

Sticky Squares

100 g bar of Cadbury's Bournville chocolate
175 g (6 oz) butter
175 g (6 oz) caster sugar
4 × size 2 eggs, separated
50 g (2 oz) ground almonds
25 g (1 oz) plain flour, sieved
FOR THE FILLING
75 g (3 oz) cream cheese
175 g (6 oz) icing sugar, sieved

a 23 cm (9-inch) square or an 18 × 28 cm
   (7 × 11 inch) rectangular microwave-proof
   dish, greased and base-lined

Melt the chocolate on DEFROST for 4 minutes. Cream the butter and sugar together really well; beat in the melted chocolate and the egg yolks. Fold in the ground almonds and sieved flour. Fold in the whisked egg whites (the mixture may look curdled at this stage). Turn the mixture into the dish and microwave on HIGH for 10 minutes. Stand for a further 10 minutes before turning on to greaseproof paper to cool.

Slice the cake horizontally through the middle. Cream the cream cheese and icing sugar until pale and smooth. Spread the filling on one layer of cake and sandwich them back together. Cut into pieces and sprinkle with icing sugar.

Makes 16–18   *Pictured on page 123*

Dreamy Chocolate Pie

FOR THE BASE
250 g (9 oz) digestive biscuits
125 g (4 oz) butter
5 ml (1 teaspoon) ground ginger
FOR THE FILLING AND DECORATION
100 g bar of Cadbury's Bournville chocolate
125 ml (¼ pint) milk
1 lemon or small orange
10 ml (2 teaspoons) gelatine
2 eggs, separated
25 g (1 oz) caster sugar
142 ml (¼ pint) whipping cream
a packet of Cadbury's milk chocolate Buttons

a 23 cm (9-inch), fluted, loose-based flan tin
a piping bag and star pipe

Crush the biscuits quite coarsely. Melt the butter on HIGH for 1 minute and stir in the biscuits and ground ginger. Press the mixture over the base and up the sides of the flan tin, then chill.

Break up the chocolate and heat it with the milk in a fairly large bowl on DEFROST for about 8 minutes until the chocolate has melted. Stir every 2 minutes. Finely grate the fruit rind and add to the milk with the juice (the mixture may curdle but it does not matter). Sprinkle in the gelatine and leave to dissolve. Whisk the egg yolks and sugar until pale in colour, whisk into the chocolate milk and leave in a cold place until on the point of setting. Whisk the egg whites stiffly. Lightly whip a little of the cream and fold both into the thickening custard. Pour the filling on to the biscuit base and leave to set overnight.

Carefully lift out of the flan tin and decorate the top with piped whipped cream and chocolate Buttons.

Serves 8   *Pictured on page 119*

Moist Tea Loaf

Keep one ready for use in the freezer.

300 g (10 oz) dried mixed fruit
200 ml (7 fl oz) strong tea
100 g bar of Cadbury's Bournville chocolate
50 g (2 oz) dark soft brown sugar
175 g (6 oz) self-raising wholemeal flour
1 ripe banana

a 1 kg (2 lb) microwave-proof loaf-shaped dish,
*   greased and strip-lined*

Mix the fruit and tea together in a bowl and then microwave on REHEAT for 7 minutes. Break up the chocolate and stir in until melted. Beat in the sugar, flour and mashed banana and then turn the mixture into the dish. Microwave on an upturned plate on HIGH for 7 minutes, rotating the dish every 2 minutes. Leave to stand for a good 5 minutes before turning out to cool on a rack covered with cling film. Serve in slices lightly spread with butter; a fruit cheese is also good.

Serves 6–8

Plantation Loaf Cake

A truly moist loaf that keeps well. It looks a bit rough and ready but that is part of its charm. Bananas and chocolate go particularly well together.

FOR THE CAKE
2 small ripe bananas
125 g (4 oz) soft margarine
125 g (4 oz) dark soft brown sugar
5 ml (1 teaspoon) vanilla essence
2 eggs
40 ml (2 tablespoons) milk
100 g bar of Cadbury's Dairy Milk milk chocolate
175 g (6 oz) self-raising flour
2.5 ml (½ teaspoon) bicarbonate of soda
TO COMPLETE
2 small bananas
10 ml (2 teaspoons) lemon juice
50 g (2 oz) icing sugar, sieved
50 g (2 oz) ground almonds
100 g bar of Cadbury's Dairy Milk milk chocolate
20 ml (1 tablespoon) milk

a 1 kg (2 lb) microwave-proof, loaf-shaped dish,
*   greased and strip-lined*

For the cake, mash the bananas and then beat them with the margarine, sugar and essence until the mixture is light. Gradually add the eggs and milk. Cut each square of chocolate into four and fold into the mixture with the sieved dry ingredients. Turn into the prepared dish and microwave on HIGH for 7 minutes, rotating the dish a couple of times. Leave to stand for 5 minutes before turning out on to a wire tray covered with cling film.

Make the filling by mashing one banana with half the lemon juice. Fold in the sieved icing sugar and ground almonds. Slice the cooled cake in half through the centre, spread with filling and then sandwich back together.

Melt the chocolate in a bowl on DEFROST for 3 minutes. Stir until it is quite smooth and then beat in the milk, working hard until the icing thickens and is glossy. (The icing may look wrong but keep beating until it is thick enough – it does work.) Spread over the top of the cake. Decorate with thin slices of banana dipped in the remaining lemon juice.

Tip: You can use really ripe, black bananas in the cake itself, the colour does not matter.

Serves 6

Plantation Loaf Cake; Sticky Squares (page 121)

Micro-Chocolate Cheesecake

FOR THE BASE
50 g (2 oz) soft margarine
50 g (2 oz) caster sugar
1 egg
50 g (2 oz) self-raising flour
40 ml (2 tablespoons) milk
80 ml (4 tablespoons) rum
80 ml (4 tablespoons) fruit juice
FOR THE TOPPING
450 g (1 lb) cream cheese
75 g (3 oz) caster sugar
3 eggs
125 ml (¼ pint) milk
200 g bar of Cadbury's Bournville chocolate
75 g (3 oz) butter
142 ml (¼ pint) whipping cream

a 25 cm (10-inch), shallow or 20 cm (7½- or 8-inch),
*   deep, microwave-proof dish, greased and base-lined*

Make the sponge base first by beating the margarine,

sugar, egg, flour and the milk well together. Spread the cake mixture evenly over the base of the dish. Microwave on HIGH for 4 minutes, rotating after 2 minutes. Mix the rum and fruit juice together (or use all fruit juice) and soak the sponge whilst still warm. Use half the quantity of liquid for the smaller cheesecake.

To make the topping, beat the cream cheese and sugar together until smooth, gradually beat in the eggs and the milk. Make some chocolate curls for the decoration (page 12). Melt the remaining chocolate with the butter on DEFROST for 3 minutes and then stir until really smooth; cool before beating into the cheese mixture. Carefully pour over the base. Microwave on HIGH for 13 minutes, rotating every 3 minutes unless using a turntable. Leave in the dish to cool before turning on to a board covered with cling film.

When cold, invert on to a plate. Spread the top with lightly whipped cream and decorate simply with the chocolate curls. Keep cool until required.

Serves 8

Hot Noggin

275 ml (½ pint) milk
60 ml (3 tablespoons) Cadbury's drinking chocolate
40 ml (2 tablespoons) whisky
1 egg, beaten lightly
a little ground cinnamon
a Cadbury's Flake

Measure the milk, drinking chocolate and whisky into the jug. Whisk together and then heat on HIGH for 3 minutes, stirring half-way through. Whisk in the egg and strain if desired. Pour the drink into tumblers, sprinkle with cinnamon and crushed Flake.

Serves 2

Micro-Chocolate Cheesecake; Criss-Cross Sponge Pudding (page 121)

Fondue

200 g bar of Cadbury's Bournville chocolate
142 ml (¹/₄ pint) double cream
60 ml (3 tablespoons) honey or golden syrup
a selection of prepared fresh fruit
a family box of Cadbury's Flake

Break up the chocolate and put into a bowl with the cream and honey or syrup. Microwave on HIGH for 1 minute; stir and heat again for a further 30 seconds. Serve in small fondue pots, if you have them, with a colourful selection of fresh fruit, using fondue forks if available; cocktail sticks make an adequate alternative.

Also dip in the Flake – they are lovely dripping with fondue.

Tip: Add any of the following; marshmallows, crushed soft mints, instant coffee, 2 mashed bananas, ice cream – serving the fondue before the ice cream melts – and last but not least, a little rum, brandy or liqueur. There really is no limit to the number of variations you can create – have fun!

Serves 4 or more

$Index$

To help you identify the recipes, the following codes have been added to the main entries : **LC** (Large Cake); **SC** (Small Cakes); **BB** (Biscuits and Bakes); **HP** (Hot Puddings); **CD** (Cold Desserts). Variations and alternative names are also listed; these are distinguished by having only an initial capital letter.